Live in your new story

ANNE & AMANDA

'There is no greater agony than bearing an untold story inside you.'

Maya Angelou

Dedicated to:

Our Dads.

Thank you for the opportunities you extended us both by changing your stories. We are the result of your hard work and dedication.

STORIES USED IN THIS BOOK

The stories in this book are fictional or personal stories told from the author's understanding and perspective and not from a definitive statement of the lives of others. Note, some stories have been embellished to illustrate a concept.

BE ADVISED

This workbook provides general information to help you on your journey of wellbeing. It is not intended to offer psychological help for any diagnosed physical, emotional or medical issues. If you become distressed when reading or answering the questions contained in this workbook, please seek professional help.

It should be noted that the information provided is current as at date of publishing. Neither the authors, nor those responsible for the contents, or production of this book, shall be liable for any damages arising here from. In summation, any application of these contents is the responsibility of the reader.

ISBN: 978-1-63625-613-9

All enquiries regarding this publication and speaking engagements to: www.changeyourstory.events

Cover & Book Design by: Kellie Book Design
www.kelliemaree.com

Contents

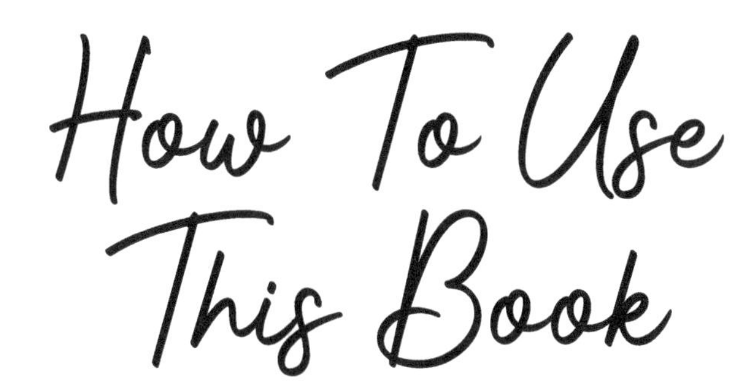

Anne and Amanda have helped lots of people leave their unhelpful stories where they belong – in the past. As you read this book, our wish is that your heart becomes more fully awake to your new story. The content of this book comprises of four main themes.

Identity

Beauty

Authority

Self-Compassion

Each theme is written from two narratives with their unique perspectives. This book was co-written for this reason. As you move through the book, take your time to reflect on the author's perspective. At the end of each chapter, you will find some prompts to help you journal through your perspective. You will also be introduced to some creative exercises to help you integrate the subject matter.

We are all on a journey of discovery together. One thing that we want to help you with is to read this book safely. To do this, we would recommend you read and participate in the following meditation created to help you build a safe place as you discover and unpack some of your narratives through the stories, insights and revelations in this book.

Introd

'We all get lost once in a while, sometimes by choice, sometimes due to forces beyond our control. When we learn what it is our soul needs to learn, the path presents itself. Sometimes we see the way out but wander further and deeper despite ourselves; the fear, the anger or the sadness preventing us returning. Sometimes we prefer to be lost and wandering, sometimes it's easier. Sometimes we find our own way out. But regardless, always, we are found.'

Cecelia Ahern

Wake up Deborah

'Once upon a time, there was a little girl named Deborah who dreamed of becoming the president of the whole entire world. Well maybe the mayor of her town. She wanted to be a prophet and judge who sat underneath the trees at council, helping her community become strong.

In her family and tradition, those roles were only for the wise Fathers. She couldn't help it though. She imagined standing on stages and speaking with authority, helping people. She wanted to help the whole town.

Leadership as a child came naturally to her. She walked through life confidently knowing that one day she would do something that would be written into the annals of time.

One day she would stand strong in influential places.

One day.

Was it bad to think this way?

She wanted her story to be told. One that inspired others to live beyond their every day lives.

As she grew older, she began to work out how the world worked; she didn't want to make her dreams seem too big. One morning, (she was now ten years old) she lay on the grass with butterflies circling her mind.

The friendship she had made with the forest was her daily delight.

Taking deep breaths full of ideas, new possibilities and changing the story of her people, she practised her speeches and saw herself walking through crowds of people. She delighted in chatting with God and hearing from him, gaining insight and stories of the future of how she would help others.

She was so excited about the possibility of tomorrow.

Things changed that summer; shadows began to take over her mind. She wondered whether those whispers from God under the tree were just her imagination playing tricks on her.

She was unsure of where the fear and shame began. She felt so isolated and alone, no one understanding her motive. Always second-guessing her thoughts.

Being left out of games at school was one of those times where she felt the early stings of rejection. Other children telling her she was too bossy, too much and shouting, 'you always want to be the person in charge.'

These stories marked her confidence. She wondered if all her dreams of making a difference, having a life with meaning to help others, were all just fantasy. Where she used to confidently walk into rooms and sit with friends under the trees in the afternoon, she now wished she could fade into the background.

'Not good enough' they chanted, as she walked past the oval.

'Not pretty enough' she overheard, sitting quietly in the bathroom waiting for the lunch bell to ring.

'Not smart enough' she remembered her teacher saying just loud enough for her to place it in her memory bank of lies.

'Not thin enough' she read the report card from the ballet examiner.

Now as she lay on the grass the butterflies didn't seem to fly in her imagination as carefree as they once did. Reoccurring words written deeply into the playground of her mind replaced the little flying fancies, those pretty butterflies.

She thought maybe if she went to sleep, if she slept a long time through life, then maybe the stories that haunted her in the daytime, wouldn't hurt so much.

Sleep took away the pain, of not enough-ness.

Sleep made her think of less, not wanting to become something more.

Sleep comforted her stories and made her shrink away, hoping nobody would notice.

Softly, a voice came through her sleep, haunting her to change her story.'

> *'Wake up, wake up, Deborah! Wake up,*
> *wake up, break out in song!'*
> *Judges 5:12 (NIV)*

This is a fictional representation of the story of Deborah as a child. She is one of the most influential women of the Bible. As a Prophet and Judge, Deborah was said to hear God's voice and share his word with others.

Do you ever feel like something is missing?

Is the story of your life leaving you wanting more?

You possess a significant story.

The life you have dreamed of, those things that come naturally to you, they are a part of your future story.

This fictionalised version of the childhood life of Deborah, a Judge from scripture, is an opportunity for us to see with perspective what it would have taken for her to step into her leadership story. Her story was recorded for generations upon generations to be inspired by.

The interesting part about her story is the way she stepped into places of influence in a culture and society that believed women could not play these leadership roles.

What did it take for Deborah to change her story?

We all have experiences in our childhood like Deborah dreaming of her future. Places where we have believed other people's expectations of us. Beliefs where we remain stuck.

Every one of us is a walking catalogue of helpful and unhelpful narratives. There are moments within our own stories where we get stuck and the easiest options sometimes can be to sleepwalk through life, to numb ourselves from the pain.

We can be so deep in these archives that it's hard to unravel the yarns of old. We promise ourselves that something will change but year after year we walk the same, familiar path.

It's natural for us to believe old stories because they were told to us by the people that matter.

At some point in time, we have agreed with these stories about us and made them our own. Stories of validation empower us. Stories of disapproval create wounds that may never completely heal. But what if, instead of attacking ourselves for living in myths we didn't create, we could catch, contain, and transform these erroneous tales. In this way we can relieve future generations from walking in our old story.

This is our invitation to you today...

Awake

Live in Your New Story.

Awake to Safety

'When you know how to return to safety,
the world won't scare you as much.'

Anne Galambosi

Awakening is a reconstructive process. Unhelpful old stories are torn down and exposed for the lies they contain, leaving a space for the new story to grow. This can be an exhilarating and freeing experience, and a little confronting at times.

The potential for confrontation and disruption is why we ask that you complete this exercise before reading any further. It is a simple meditation that helps you return to safety within yourself any time you feel a bit unsettled.

A recording of this meditation is available at www.changeyourstory.events

Alternatively, you may wish to record the following script yourself on your phone and listen back when needed.

Let's begin by becoming aware of your body.
Relax your body by focusing on your breathing. Gentle cool breaths in.
Then, notice the slow, long, warm breath leaving your body.
Breathe in slowly and gently.
Each time you exhale allow yourself to relax a little deeper.

That's it...
let go and relax...
Gently inhale...
Slowly exhale and relax a little further.
Scan your body from the top of your head right down to your toes.

Search for any tension and let it go.
Relax your eyebrows, relax your jaw.
Relax your shoulders, relax your hands.
Melt into the chair.
Relax your feet.

If you are finding it hard to relax... it maybe that your body and mind are trying to protect you from trusting the process.
Take a moment...to honour your body...and mind...
They have done their best to protect you, now... and in the past

Now say to your body and mind, 'Thank you for protecting me... It's ok. I am choosing to trust this process, and I will always be in control.
Just as a loud noise can wake me up, my subconscious will let me know if I am in physical danger. It is safe to relax at this moment. I will do my best to relax and let go a little more. Letting all the tension go out of my body.'

Imagine a place of safety.
A place where you have felt safe before.
Perhaps it's a room in your house, or the ocean, the forest, or somewhere else.
Wherever that safe place is...
Imagine you are in that safe place right now...
How does it feel? Focus on that feeling.
Here is your safe place. Your body can let go even more because you know you are safe.

Imagine feelings of happiness in your safe place. You are with someone kind to you;
It may be God, a person or a pet, and they are comforting you.
It is so peaceful here in your safe place.
No worries or cares.
You are soaking up the peace into your body.
You hear soothing, peaceful music
You can see all around you in this safe place.

You will also notice here, in your safe place, there is door back to the present moment.
You can leave your safe place whenever you feel ready, knowing that any time you feel overwhelmed, you can come back to this place.
You can come back here to this peaceful place in your mind any time you want to.

Rewriting My Story

Amanda

'Time is growing short. There are unexplored adventures ahead of you. You can't live the rest of your life worried about what other people think. You were born worthy of love and belonging. Courage and daring are coursing through you. You were made to live and love with your whole heart. It's time to show up and be seen.'

Brene Brown

The wind was wild and relentless yesterday as I walked the beach, just a few minutes from my bungalow home. If you had told me ten years earlier that I would one day run to the beach at sunset with my little family in tow, I would have said 'Impossible!'

As I bobbed in the murky sea, reflecting on the change of narrative that has occurred over the last decade, I smiled with gratitude. The rewriting of my story changed my life.

I grew up in a little seaside town, with two parents who tried desperately to provide for their three children. They worked hard with many different businesses and could often be found awake late into the night, dreaming about tomorrow.

Both my parents came with stories from their childhood that impacted the way they parented their new family. My Dad grew up in a rural setting with a big family. He had dyslexia, experienced domestic violence, and poverty was the plotline of his upbringing. My Mum lost her Dad to cancer when she was just fifteen, and the pain impacted her deeply.

My story was a pretty standard story. You know, growing up in the suburbs, with friends and birthday parties, a BMX bike and dolls tucked inside my bed covers.

A childhood that was full of lots of creativity and delight. However, there are significant parts of it I can't remember. It is like someone blacked out my memories with a big black texta and I can no longer see what is underneath.

Although there are parts I can't remember, those deep secrets I held close to my chest, buried as a small child hoping that I could forget them. Outside of those blank pages, everything else was pretty average. I felt ordinary. No one needs to hear about it. It was just a standard Australian life.

Yet I stumbled across scriptures such as;

> *God rewrote the text of my life when I opened*
> *the book of my heart to his eyes.*
> *Psalm 18:24 (MSG)*

I realised, during a season of awakening, that God designed me to live a life of purpose, even amid my everyday, ordinary suburban life. We can't change what happened to us but we can 'rewrite' the narrative of the story. I was a teenager, and I loved my family, but I needed to move far away to discover the depth of purpose in my own story and life. I could not wait to leave the seaside town from my childhood, vowing never to return.

I studied at university in a big city and found myself in the roar of creative pursuit from my new, exciting urban setting. Drinking, drug taking, and exploring my ideologies and foundations were the art of my youth. Amid theatre companies, and late-night singing in bars, I somehow found myself tucked in the pocket of my friend's spiritual journey. She invited me into the conversation she was having with God - one full of life, intention and beautiful healing.

I encountered a youth awakening that drew me into its tide — young people singing to God, rather than pub songs, with drunken karaoke.

We would rock up to leadership development courses in the afternoon with debates about theology.

In the day, I would hang out with the theatre kids at university, who were smoking and drinking towards creative clarity. At night I would stand alongside young people shouting towards the 'Great Unknown', asking God to show them a new way. The juxtaposition of my college life was jagged — church worship at night and universalism during the day.

This season was the rewriting of my story. I opened my heart to a new way, and suddenly some of those blank pages began to fill. Like a mystery puzzle, with words flying from one memory to another, I realized there were secrets in my perfect childhood that had held me captive to my past.

Moments, whispers and boundaries crossed, that held my heart captive in fear — people who told me things that were not true, about the way I looked. I didn't realize that these blank pages from my past were still informing my future. They had created a scaffold that locked me in a holding pattern, keeping me stuck.

Telling me I was ugly.

Shouting in silence that I would never have a family.

Begging me to keep quiet and tell no one.

Never go to the beach again, the place were those stories were created.

Stay away from love it is not safe.

Stay cautious and suspicious of intimate relationships with men.

The rewriting that became apparent was a changing of the story that was written on my heart. This scripture from Corinthians in the Bible wooed me away to explore the power of changing the story of my life and the difficult things that have happened.

> *'For your very lives are our 'letters of recommendation,' permanently engraved on our hearts, recognized and read by everybody. As a result of our ministry, you are living letters written by Christ, not with ink but by the Spirit of the living God—not carved onto stone tablets but on the tablets of tender hearts.'*
> *2 Corinthians 3:2-3 (TPT)*

This is the beauty of co-authoring our lives with God; He helps to take those blacked out words, that people have written on our hearts with texta, and rewrites our story into one of living ink.

My heart was stuck because I held questions about what was right and wrong. People had led my heart towards things that were adult concepts, and the shame that hid on those blanked-out pages froze my heart in fear. As I recalled some of the memories from those forgotten secrets, my life ached and grieved a childhood lost.

The accent of shame shadowed the way I learned to speak to myself.

Writing became my refuge in this season of awakening — seasons of clarity like this wake up even the parts of us that want to stay asleep. I made vows to myself, as a teenager, that I would never trust anyone with my heart and that no one could know those hidden secrets from my childhood.

Remembering that I was ugly, I was unlovable, and I loathed my body. My childhood stories held score in my body. Although there were blank pages in my mind, my physical body held onto the pain viscously.

These blank pages contained truths that I wanted no one to ever speak of again. The awakening unlocked the vows I spoke to protect myself from being hurt again. Vows I had made to myself as a teenager, that I would never trust anyone with my heart and that no one could know these hidden secrets from my childhood. But my story was being rewritten with every encounter I had with God.

The thing about changing the narratives of our lives is this; we need to show up to the work of changing our story! We show up through journalling, counselling, and finding like-minded people who are interested in the work of self-compassion.

I think sometimes we are told that healing happens in an instant, but I have found when we surrender to its process that it happens over a season. That is the power of awakening. Slowly allowing God to rewrite our story. Like the days that I wrote, and tried to change the tone of my narrative, but some days it felt like I was going in circles. I didn't want anyone to know my secrets, or to come close, and at the same time, I was terrified that I was not enough to find someone who would write a love story with me.

Despite all the healing, my soul was gripped with fear believing that I would live the rest of my life alone. I found journalling to be a powerful tool to find the stories that I had believed from other people. I wanted the words of our Eternal Author to shape my life. I needed to believe in the new story and see a Divine adventure calling me towards a life of influence. I have sat on counsellor's couches and stood in prayer lines. I sang my heart out to worship songs and remembered that my heart's tenderness was not a flaw but a superpower. There was a rewriting of my story happening deep within the very core and foundation of my belief system.

There was an old story: I will always be alone.

The new story: I am safe.

Another old story: I am not good enough.

The new story: I am loved.

That's why my story from the beach, in this season, brings deep gratitude. This coming year I celebrate ten years of being married to a man who came alongside and helped me write a new story of a family together. There were new parts of the healing that needed to happen in partnership with someone who wanted to hang out with just me.

Miraculously I fell pregnant on our honeymoon, even though doctors had told me that I would never fall pregnant, due to the damage from a burst appendix and losing my ovary.

Yesterday as I walked the wildness of the beach, I saw my two children bouncing together, smiling back at me amid the wind and waves. They waved and played happily, neither knowing that the same sand we stood on, was some of the places I vowed I would never return.

Some of my blanked out memories were from the shores of that very beach. The rewriting of this story took me to a new memory formed in this seaside town, these dunes, and these waters.

I had returned to the seaside town that I thought I would never return to, my children go to the very same school that I attended as a child. On some days a flash of memory and insight return and I have learnt to allow those memories to come, so I can hold the little girl who offers these precious memories as gifts back to the adult me. I start to see things differently like God is opening my eyes to new days and new stories for the future.

I tell her she is going to be okay.
I tell her she is not in trouble.
I tell her she is safe.

I show her that God has rewritten our story together.

> *'He touched their eyes and said, 'Become what you believe.' It happened. They saw.'*
> *Matthew 9:29 (MSG)*

Even yesterday as we swam in the ocean, memories came flooding back, and I said thank you. I can't change the things that happened to me, but I can reframe the way I speak to myself about the identity and voice that those experiences formed in my heart and life.

There is a garden that is bursting into life within our minds. The seeds that we plant there become fruit. Although all of our stories are very different in content, we each have a story to tell. One that is shaped by the things we remember about our childhood and also the things that we have forgotten.

The power of our partnership with Christ is the capacity to change the way we speak to our future selves and the beauty of the promise He brings for our greater tomorrow.

So here I am on the midst of a new season and chapter, and I am wondering what future we will write together for tomorrow. Your story has a purpose. Those difficult things that happened to you even though they made your story hard, they can be reformed to become the strength of foundation for the tenacity of your resilience.

Change your story, my friend; it is time for a new chapter.

We all have a story, and I believe that there is somebody in the world who needs your story. As we write for recovery and self-awareness, there is a moment of growth that happens as we awaken to the possibility found in our story. Reflect on the questions below and take the time to bring value to your story and its underlying power. Grab a pen and paper. Now is an opportunity for you to write for insight and discovery.

In what ways does your story matter?

In what ways could your story inform, help or encourage others?

When have you told your story to another person?

How do you feel talking about yourself?

Iden

'When we share our stories, we are reminded of the humanity in each other. When we take the time to understand each other's stories, we become more forgiving, empathetic and more inclusive.'

Michelle Obama

The power of identity in the narratives of our story is undeniable. As we understand where stories have held us stuck in our life, we can begin to see the reshaping and reforming of our identity and where we get our sense of self.

In this section of this book Amanda and Anne take you on a journey where they are unpacking their life stories to discover where they have based their identity. We all have a worldview, which began with our parent's insights and belief. The history of our family of origin also shapes our understanding of the world.

A key component of our awakening begins with understanding our identity and also what shapes our worldview.

Come on a journey of discovery with us and let's change our stories together.

Awake to Identity

Anne

'Identity is a prison you can never escape, but the way to redeem your past is not to run from it, but to try to understand it, and use it as a foundation to grow.'

Jay Z

Understanding how you came to be you is the first step in creating a new identity story. Identities are shaped by the voices of our ancestors. We reach adulthood and yet their messages are so ingrained that we wouldn't even think that we might function differently or without them. So, in spite of reaching an age where we break away, we actually bring them with us. We are an extension of what our mother and father have been taught and teach us, until we become more self-aware. Our family histories have such a powerful effect on our identity development that when we get older, it is necessary for us to separate ourselves from the voices of our families to form an independent and harmonious relationship between our inner self and the world.

I've chosen to share some intimate details from my mother's and father's childhood experiences. Detail has been created by my imagination from the pieces of their stories that I know. These examples are intended to show how wounds and joys are passed down from generation to generation, informing our response to the world, and our place within it.

His Story // Agra India, 1932

It's 6 pm and will soon be dark.

'Be strong,' she said.

Don't feel is what he hears.

On the stone steps of St John's orphanage and boarding school, his three-year-old brother Peter stands beside him as they watch her step into the car without a backward glance. At five years of age, he has no comprehension of abandonment—just a stiff upper lip. He grabs his brother's hand and squeezes it tight. Pete is screaming. He determines that nothing will happen to Pete as much as it is up to him.

Guiding hands pull him in toward the big doors, no point in running. Escape will never be an option. There is nobody to take them in.

The years pass slowly. There are the poor boarders and the rich. He and his brother are among the poor. His dorm is on the rundown side of the orphanage. The rich are on the maintained side. His bed is bare and hard. He has no idea what their beds are like, separated from them by a big red line. Having suffered plenty of painful punishments from minor infractions he learns to never dare go over that red line.

They all meet in the classroom and this is where he thrives. He turns over his returned exam paper to reveal a predictable A+ in the top right corner. He receives no praise. His efforts are invisible. The school bell rings. The long hot days lead to extended lunch breaks. He feels his brother's hand tug his tattered shirt. Pete's found a beaten up, empty can.

'We can play soccer!' he shouts.

This rare find fills his whole body with pleasure. They kick it around for the whole lunchtime. Laughter echoes in the dirt playground as other penniless boys join in, sparking a moment of happiness.

Sunday comes. The sweets van rolls in and the children spy the array of syrupy candies lined up on the counter. The rich boarders jostle for a place in line, rich boys of varying age laughing and enjoying the banter. With shiny coins in their hands, there are no thoughts for the unseen boarders. He waits to the side with his brother, hoping for coins that might fall to the ground and roll toward them.

It never happens.

Another Sunday comes. The sweets van rolls in and yet again they can only watch on. Something snaps inside him. With no thought to the severe punishment that the crime would incur, he announces: 'Come on, let's go.'

He scurries around to the back of the van with his brother. 'You go cause a fight with the boys at the front of the line,' he instructs. 'Yell a lot first, ok?' Asking Pete to kneel down, he uses his back to climb onto the side of the van, then waves him on. He sees his brother's unwavering trust in his wide smile.

He watches as Pete strides toward the line and accuses loudly, 'I saw you push into the line, Adesh.'

'Did not!'

'Did so,' Pete goads. 'Samuel should be getting his sweets now, not you.'

'Hey!' Samuel says to Adesh, shoving him aside. 'Get to the back of the line and wait your turn.' Adesh lands a heavy punch into Samuel. And the fight is on!

By this time, he is within reaching distance of the brightly coloured, mouth-watering sweets.

Frantically, the merchant leaves his post to pull the boys apart. He locked eyes with Pete, who is grinning from ear to ear. It fills him with the last bit of courage he needs to reach around. The sweets feel softer than he thought they would. They crumble slightly in his hand, and he relaxes his grip a little.

Touching his bare feet softly to the ground, he hurries around to the back of the van. Within seconds Pete's hand is pulling his open. Four treats coat his skin in sticky deliciousness. One rose, two light green and one smashed yellow treat glisten up at them. The heavenly waft of ghee-laden sugar and spice makes his mouth water. He glances at Pete to see triumph written all over his face, and he knows that he is his hero. And, in that moment, Pete is his hero. Pete is the only one who is there for him. Their noses almost collide as they move in closer for a better whiff of cardamon.

Right then, it happens.

The most glorious moment. The sugar syrup melts on his tongue. The roasted nuts crumble as the milky almond paste swirls around his mouth. Their smiles toward each other reveal the gelatinous mass sticking around their teeth, too scared to swallow lest the moment end.

Darkness comes. Bedclothes put on. Lights out. He leans down over the edge of his bunk bed to his brother below.

'No-one saw us today, you know.'

'I know,' he giggles back.

Sleep comes easy.

He dreams of his mother.

He dreams of her lovely face as she walks toward the open door where he is waiting for her. A long white car waits behind her on the road. He takes her hand and they run down the stairs where a man in a white uniform opens the car door for them.

Together they glide into the back seat and she places a big white box on his lap, bound with a bright yellow ribbon. He unlaces the ribbon and opens the lid. Rows of delicious treats fill the box, all the colours of the rainbow. She responds to his look of amazement.

'Yes, they are all for you.'

Ravenously, he shoves as many into his mouth as he can. Her laughter fills the car and fills his heart too. In the rear vision mirror, he sees the driver's eyes gleaming back at him as he starts the engine. He glances past his mother's beautiful face through the car window, and then it occurs to him. His wonderful dream is turning into a nightmare.

Panicking, he shrieks, 'Wait for my brother!'

With an effortless smile she says, 'Only you are coming with me, my darling.'

He wakes with his heart pounding in his chest. The ceiling looms above him in the oppressive darkness.

Her Story // Masnill Holland, 1940

Toes toasting while she watches the fire glow, she can hear her brothers playfully teasing each other and it makes her smile. Not a care in the world lives in her house. Pots casually knock together while the evening meal is prepared. Music lightly fills the atmosphere and mingles with cigar smoke. She hears a wooden spoon scraping the bottom of the pot as her mother gently rocks her brand-new sister. Within moments it all changes. The safety of her childhood home was never to abide with her again. She hears the radio crackle and the volume is turned up. All the houses in the street echoing the same news. Germany has invaded Poland.

Face ashen, her father returns to the loungeroom with quick instructions to her mother and eldest brother. Her father had been warned by a neighbour that the Germans had announced a forced labour policy and are coming for eligible men. Panic replaces peace, danger replaces safety, and anxiety replaces predictability. Above the noise of the wailing baby, her parents discuss all the options. They scurry down to the cellar with haste to prepare a place for her father and brother to hide. Taking a long look at her father and brother's frightened faces, she's the last one to climb the stairs back to the kitchen.

During those war years, she lived in constant anxiety above the place where her two male protectors hid, terrified that they would be found and imprisoned. Time after time, soldiers imposed entry into their home, taking their food, her favourite doll, her mum's wedding band; anything they wanted. Once, she was taking bread down to the cellar when they came. They all froze. With one hand over her mouth and another around her body, her father held her fear captive and still. She watched the bread knife balancing precariously on the edge of the table desperately hoping it would not fall and expose them all. It could have fallen; it happened not to. Finally, she heard the footfall of the soldiers disappear on the path as they left her home. She let out a breath she didn't know she was holding.

After the war, with her father and brother released from their cellar prison, they were once again a family. However, the fear that war would break out again meant that things were never the same. They decided to leave.

When she steps off the boat in Australia, the stifling heat somehow intensifies the grief of leaving behind all that she had known. What she would have given to go back home into the sweet, cool air of Holland! They moved into their first flat. She says to anyone who will listen, 'If there was a bridge, I would walk back to Holland right now.' She feels self-conscious all the time. Nothing is familiar. Living with the decision her parents chose for her, she tries to enter this new culture. Even the simplest of tasks, like trying to buy something, is challenging.

Next, to be served at the shop counter, she is terrified of saying the wrong words.

The shopkeeper says, 'Yes, what would you like?'

She searches her mind for the English word for milk, but it escapes her no matter how hard she tries. Red heat rises up her neck and warms her newly acquired freckles, forged by the burning sun her skin's not used to. She runs. Her hair whips around her face and sticks to the tears streaming down her cheeks. Safely back at home, her father's face is full of compassion. He soothes her in her native tongue and then sets off back to the shop to get the milk for her. Secure in the walls of her family home, she settles, busying herself by helping her mother prepare for the other new migrants who continually visit them.

Full bellies and thankful hearts retire to the lounge that evening. At the end of a long night of dishes and listening to funny stories about 'us Dutchies' being misunderstood, she tiptoes into her bedroom. The sheets are crisp, and she finds her sister has warmed her side of the bed. As she slides in, her sister stirs and wriggles in close and it makes her heart warm.

Mum wakes her up in the morning. 'You're needed by a Dutch family with ten children. Can you go now please and help the mother?'

Again, the liberty of youth is interrupted for her as she takes on a familiar adult role. She could never imagine the freedom to say no. This is simply what she is expected to do: sacrifice for others who need help. She accepts life as it is and makes the best of things. Ten children with their cheeky grins and snotty noses. Soiled nappies don't bother her a bit. She enjoys the warm little bodies that sit in her lap as she tells stories in Dutch that she wishes she could read in English.

With all her heart, she loves her family, and is taught that she must always be on the lookout for those who need help.

My Story // Western Australia, 1999

My belly starts to tense up, a twisting eel-like sensation that obscures my ability to reason. It's the most unpleasant feeling that I know so well... shame. Self-loathing consumes every inch of my being and sleep escapes me. No particular reason or event has triggered this experience; it's just my way of being. The emptiness of the night and its hollow darkness provokes my mind to fill up with a flow of disparaging truths: *what meaning could my life possibly bring to this world? I have nothing to offer, in fact, I'm only a drain in every relationship, people only suffer my existence because they're stuck with me.* It's not only the night that sets off my relentless shame. I only need to spend time alone for the feeling to come upon me. The days, full of distraction, are easier.

To self-soothe the tension inside my body, I turn to my own unhealthy way of escape... idealistic fantasies. What will I imagine tonight? I see myself walking onto a stage where all the people I want to impress are waiting for the melody to begin. My song has a bell-like quality that fills the room, leaving people in awe. I'm taller, pretty and desirable. Or, perhaps I am buried in the ground, and people I love are gathered around the graveside peering down. I can see who is sad that I am not around anymore, and it makes me feel wanted. Or maybe, thousands of people are sitting cross-legged on an expanse of grass as I impart incredible, life-changing words that transform their lives forever. The distraction of fantasy offers an alternate consciousness; one where I am momentarily free from self-loathing. If the negative emotions I have about myself are replaced effectively enough with the fantasy of who I wished I was, sleep will come.

Understanding the connection

It is not surprising that being able to distinguish ourselves from the people we're related to is a difficult task. When we are young, we perceive our parents as an extension of the self rather than separate human beings. Thus, the first step to forming our own identity is to unfasten the connection between their unhelpful stories and our own. My story didn't start with my conception. It started with the experiences of two, who live in me. Many of my positive and negative attributes could not exist without the impact of his story and her story. If I go back in time, I can see how my inner child has soaked up many moments of self-loathing that have led to my narrative.

A STORY OF ME WITH HIM.

I was about ten when I broke his rule. Using a long round stick, I could just about reach the container on the shelf. I jumped, trying to bring the container closer but knocked a tin of paint off the shelf. Paralysed, I watched it land on the garage floor. The lid bent on impact, and the white paint oozed onto the grey concrete. I scooped it up as best I could, but the evidence could not be erased. Sitting in the loungeroom, I heard his car and then the garage roller door. He was home. Before long, his fingers bit into my arm as he dragged me down to the garage. He hits me three or four times. I see her standing, helpless in the doorway, screaming at him to stop.

When I understand his story, I begin to realise that he parented from a place of pain and administered discipline that usually went unquestioned in his generation. You see, I had broken his rule that says children are not allowed in the garage. The rule existed to protect us from tools and chemicals that might harm us. He was enforcing this rule in the only way his history had taught him to: severely. And in light of his boarding house upbringing, it's understandable that this form of punishment seemed appropriate to him. But it was not. This story, along with many other similar incidents, helped create such a harsh inner critic within me. Severe self-punishment became my response to real or imagined failure.

A part of his story has become my story.

A STORY OF ME WITH HER.

Kneeling on a folded towel, I pull myself along with my hands as I hum to myself. A soft yellow cloth glides easily over the skirting board curves.

'Leave a little dust on the skirting today.'

I look up at her perplexed.

'No matter how hard I clean, it will never be good enough,' she explains. 'Visitors are coming and I want them to find some dust so they'll have something to talk about on their way home.' We laugh together at her cheekiness, however we both know that this bit of dust can be the only flaw they find.

She asks, 'Start on the kitchen floor now please.'

My sisters have already started on the bathroom and laundry tiles. We all know how to clean a floor. The first step is to cover the surface with the white powder from the long green tin. Dipping a scrubbing brush into a bucket of hot water, begin to swish the powder up into to a paste so it makes a foamy lather. Once the scrubbing is complete, boil the kettle. Carefully pour the scalding water on the floor and watch the white foam dissolve. Scrape the suds away with a towel that is carefully wrapped around the end of a broom. This time round, a fine layer of residue remains, so boil the kettle once more and repeat the rinse. If there is still some residue, then I must rinse again. Then it's on hands and knees with a clean towel to dry and shine the lino to its final glory. The glory will be silently admired by the people that matter more than life itself. Family.

When I understand her story, I begin to realise she is parenting out of her historical experiences. My mother's humour and strong work ethic are evident in this story, however, it's also an example of the ridiculous standards of perfectionism that I grew up with and which later pervaded my life.

Her story also speaks of the common migrant experience. Firstly, family is everything when you don't yet fit in with others. Therefore, pleasing family means survival. Secondly, the constant humiliation caused by language barriers and by not fitting in with cultural norms leads to pushing past reasonable limits of achievement in order to feel successful. The overwhelming unwritten rule passed down from her family was be excellent, not just enough. Although striving for excellence created in me a high internal driver that has helped me accomplish many things in my life, it has also created a strong internal critic that has bullied me relentlessly. Carrying this trait has also negatively impacted all my relationships. I have been more critical with others than I would like to admit.

A part of her story has become my story.

Conscious and unconscious memories, primarily from my father's story and my mother's story, have shaped who I am. Living with a father who cut himself off from hurt with anger and punishment, and a mother who used perfectionism to ward off inferiority, developed some pretty strong negative patterns in my life. It wasn't until I was willing to engage with my reflection, that my hidden feelings and fears were identified and I could begin to change my story. Not all childhood stories were what we wanted. However, as adults, we are given the opportunity to change the script.

How Was Your Identity formed?

When I trained as a therapist, I developed a deep and complex interest in the generational patterns that replayed in my own life. Further, I wanted to figure out which patterns were the real me and which ones I adopted from others. There are many theories that explain the difference between the true, false and ideal selves. The true self represents the part of our self that belongs to us and contains our own authentic thoughts and feelings. Our false self represents the part of us that operates unconsciously and sometimes consciously, and consists of voices we have heard all our life on how to be in this world. The ideal self represents the wish to be something unattainable, which becomes a defensive armour that protects the damaged false self.

Seeing myself as not enough was a false idea about my true self. This false self drove my constant need to pursue an ideal self. As I began to identify unhelpful behaviours like rage and perfectionism, I realised that they came from my internalised father and mother scripts, which is my false self. Of course, I also had to take responsibility for how I have added to my story with my own perceptions and deceptions.

I have often had clients say to me, 'I don't feel my true self.' I usually respond by asking them if they are exhausted. Somewhat surprised by my question, they reply 'yes.' I hold up a pen and say, 'This pen weighs almost nothing, but if I had to hold it up for eight hours a day, I would be exhausted.' This analogy allows us to explore how exhausting it is to continually hold up a false self to the world. Being real is much less exhausting.

Listening for our internalised parent voices can be a valuable exercise to analyse how our false self is constructed. These ancient voices contain unwritten rules that continue to shape our stories. Myths such as, *big girls don't cry, nice girls don't do that, or sex is dirty,* are concepts that can lead us toward creating a false self because it's acceptable to our family or peers, and helps us fit in. However, maintaining the false self comes at the cost wholeness.

It's Hard to Take on a New Story

Can I trust my perception?

One of the biggest challenges in being able to detach from my old story, and live in my new story, was my inability to trust my perception of what is the right way to be. It was so hard for me to figure out, *am I being my real self, my false self, my ideal self?*

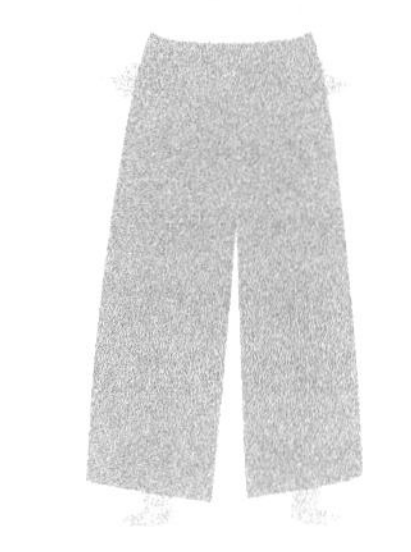

It's a tricky business to separate out the voices.

It took a willingness to examine my life daily to change my story one step at a time. Every day it's about being awake enough to discern the different voices in my head. If I am talking harshly to myself, there's my father's voice. If I'm worrying about what other people think of me, that's my mother's voice.

Our false self represents the part of us that mostly operates unconsciously and consists of voices we have heard all our lives that tell us how to be in this world. Some of those voices have been encouraging and some not. Until I developed an internal sense of self by choosing which voice I was going to listen to, I was living from my false self rather than my true self. You may need help from a friend or therapist to start to spot the false voices that you have internalised before you can tell them that they're not welcome. In that way, story by story, you start to decide which voice you're going to listen to, thereby living in your new story.

It really is possible to establish a new story. His story with me changed dramatically over the years. Alternate stories where he was generous and kind not only co-existed but became more numerous than the harsh stories until he was no longer harsh. In the end, he was my greatest encourager, my deepest listener and my beloved prayer warrior.

Can I walk away from familiarity?

It's hard to change a story that is so well-established. Old stories are familiar and known. I often tell this story to clients.

'Imagine you wave g'day to your neighbour as you leave your driveway each morning, but you don't know her. Then one day you take a trip to Italy. There on the street you notice your neighbour is walking towards you. You can't believe it! You might even hug her and say, 'Wow, fancy meeting you here! Want to go for a drink?'

Your neighbour could be a mass murderer for all you know, but here in an unfamiliar town, she is like your long-lost pal. This is why we stay stuck in old stories; at least we know them. They feel familiar. To live in your new story, you will have to take risks by exploring the unknown and by being courageous in facing your desire to change.

For me, I know that even though the journey has been difficult at times, it was worth the effort of choosing not to live out of the familiar and to live in a new story. It has been a constant and difficult path to manage my rageful self-criticism and to try not to be overly anxious about pleasing others. I am glad to be me. I have thrown out the record that played over and over in my head singing *I wish I was someone else, someone better*. I have thrown out that Linda Ronstadt record that says 'You're no good, You're no good, You're no good, Baby you're no good. I have become more content with my real self which allowed me to let go of the recurrent view of an ideal self to get to sleep. I reframed my persistent old story of perfectionism and the harsh internal critic when I realised that if I didn't allow myself to make mistakes, I would not learn. When I disentangled from my well-worn family perfection narrative, I could live in my new story that let me love my children in a way that does not connect my worth to their achievements or mistakes. Before, I would listen to the chronic voice inside my head which insisted to me that when you don't please parents you will be punished. Unfortunately, this drove much of my parenting. If only I had understood this when my children were teenagers, I wouldn't have taken it so personally when they didn't clean their bedrooms! *They weren't thinking, how can I annoy my mother!* They just had places to be, friends to see and needed time to dream. Although I have strongly adopted the common migrant value that family is everything, I no longer expect them to drop what they're doing and help me when I'm in need as a sign of their love for me.

It's difficult, but not impossible to recognise the familiar voices and change them. There are times when we slip back into customary, unhelpful patterns of thinking and behaving. Each time those parental voices are identified, there is an opportunity to stop and just observe. Gently notice, without judgement. Then make a decision to listen to or create the voice you want to hear so those unkind voices can't hurt you or others anymore.

Can I become more secure in my identity?

A strong link between the way a parent attaches to a child and their identity formation provides another reason why it is so hard to change our identity story. It's not about criticising parents, it's about coming face to face with the carry-over effect of those parenting styles. It is well-known in the therapy field that parents lean towards either a secure or insecure attachment style with their child. When the home lacks safety, a child can grow up to feel insecure. Insecure attachments to our parents fall predominantly into two types: Anxious and Avoidant [1].

Here are some common examples of how insecure parenting styles can influence our narratives.

Meet Molly. She struggled with real and imagined abandonment, unstable relationships, chronic feelings of emptiness, and inappropriate expressions of anger that stemmed from feeling anxious as a child. We traced these wounds back to experiences where her efforts to have separate thoughts and feelings from her mum or dad had massive consequences. For example, as a child, if she wanted to wear a red jumper her mum would insist she wear a blue jumper. As Molly got older, her opinions continued to be negated if they were different from her parents. This parental control left Molly with confusion. As an adult, she knew that she should feel good about being independent, yet somehow when she made decisions to suit herself, she felt bad. This is because when she wanted to do her own thing she was punished, so independence felt bad to Molly. She knows being overly dependent on others is bad, and yet it felt good. This is because whenever Molly did what her parent wanted, she was praised or accepted and that felt good.

Meet John. He internalised a different kind of insecure story, where he avoided getting too close to others. When John first came to see me, he struggled to enjoy intimate relationships because he feared that if he let people in, they would overwhelm him. In order to get a sense of self, John was often strongly assertive with others and then wondered why his relationships faded. We traced these wounds back to childhood experiences of a mum that was emotionally anxious when confronted with the needs of her children. His mother's parenting style led to him experiencing her uninvolvement one moment, and intrusiveness in another.

Understanding why you are the way you are is the first step in creating a new story. Without closer enquiry, anecdotes are just guesses at underlying reasons for identity formation. We are all caught in a spiderweb of life-long patterns that influence our current way of being. It is difficult to disentangle the self from sticky old stories that keep us immobile. We know that we have free-will to make decisions for ourselves; we know we can take control of our lives. Nevertheless, for some reason, we can feel stuck in our stories: trapped in a relationship story, trapped in an unhealthy habit story, trapped in our employment story. Whatever your story, unexplored memories that live in the mind and body can keep us frozen in ancient patterns without realising why.

Alternate Stories are Also a Part of our Identity Formation

An important step towards living in your new story is to look for the interweaving good stories. The alternate stories also define our identity. For example, just as my dad shared his precious sweets, I too will share whatever I have with those I love. My dad and uncle's love for simple pleasures, like kicking a can around, lives in me also; where I'm content with having little. Along with my internalised perfectionism from my mother, lives my drive to do things well. Her values about family is a generational blessing I see live on in my children's children. These are positive patterns that deserve as much airtime in my mind as those I am working to resolve.

The fact that you are reading this book means you have a willingness to change your identity narrative. Even though it may take determination, it is possible for you to live in your new story. Difficult, yes. Impossible, no. You've got this. You're not alone. There are several avenues of enquiry you can go down. Research and books like this one are readily available. You may want to work to uncover the source of your particular patterns that you would like to change with a therapist. Maybe you could team up with a friend who is willing to help you create an alternate story.

When we examine old stories objectively, we have more scope to decide what to claim as our new story and to establish our real identity. The intention of this chapter was not to leave you with the wistful impression of one person's childhood wounds. The aim was to share how two stories created one story in the hope that you might gain the clarity, confidence and courage to reflect on the historical narratives that distort your present.

Only you can write the story you want to live in.

Reflection

The journalling prompts below are designed to help you unpack your family stories and gain insight into your upbringing. Begin reframing your story and creating the life you truly desire.

1. What internalised unhelpful story has been around ever since you could remember, or that you're still listening to? If that story was reframed and you were able to let that story go, how would it change your life?

2. Think of a childhood story. If you could go back to that exact time and place and be your adult-self in the room as you are now, what would you say to your little self, and what would you say to the other person in the room?

3. What are some of the unwritten rules that shaped your story?

4. Now think of a current story that is a bit sticky - it might be difficult, or an attachment that's hard to let go, or something that just doesn't feel right. Write the story from the perspective of each of the people involved in the story. Think about how you could change your part in the story.

5. We all need support to live in our new story. Do you surround yourself with people that keep you stuck in your unhelpful old story or with people that champion you to live in a fabulous new story? Do you need to find more people who can support you in your new story?

6. What are some of the helpful alternate stories that deserve greater airtime in your mind?

7. What story do you want others to tell about you, and in what ways can you begin to live this story more?

Finding Our Permission

Amanda

'Every story is informed by a worldview.'

Brian Godawa

The ravens shout with dissonance as I walk through the forest of gum trees. The noise shocks me as I breathe in the wide-open spaces that bring rest to my busy mind. Each term I have been retreating to a monastery to write. The grounds of the monastery and its guesthouse are heavy with many dissonant stories. There is a small window inside the library that overlooks the dense vegetation surrounding a Spanish church. Each quarter-hour the church bells ring to herald the moving of time.

I am transported to another time, an era free of digital distractions and platforms for our ideas. Thoughts, opinions and motivations were simple back then.

Or were they?

As I sit waiting for inspiration to arise, I wonder what propelled the monks to travel across the seas to a foreign land, full of spiders and snakes, to build a Spanish monastic community and township.

There had to be a moment of clarity that called them to lean into the discomfort of pioneering a new life here. I wonder what it was like to encounter indigenous Australians in the midst of their travels, and how they spoke to one another to unravel communication from either ends of the earth. As their cultures collided, how possibly could they have understood one another?

I think about those whose land upon which I stand, the indigenous people who have walked this country for thousands of years. The times that I have not listened to their stories and the pain of pioneering here in these desert places in our nation.

The stories stolen from their families. The forgotten people, the laughter of friendships and the bitter, deep betrayal that happened in these places. The voices of those no one will listen to. I see the flags of our first nations people, the colours flowing softly in the wind in remembrance of lost lives, lost voices and lost stories.

There is a rewriting happening, and we cannot ignore it any longer. The voices of indigenous people across our land are speaking louder and louder.

The stories that have been passed down from generation to generation inform the way we see the world. This becomes the powerful force of our worldview. The pre-conceived notions that we carry into our future impact every story and narrative that we pack in our backpack of life.

There are fundamental beliefs that we all carry, that ground us and also propel us towards our tomorrow. These are our pre-conceived bias, and it is wise to question where our worldview has been formed.

The genesis of your worldview begins with the way that you have experienced life through the eyes of another.

Her Story

His Story

My Story

Our Story

Do you come from a single-parent household?

Did your parents separate or divorce?

What is the structure of your family?

How many siblings do you have?

Where did you go to school?

What is your native language?

All of our experiences frame our worldview.

The places where you feel stuck are often the places where you are holding onto obligation to a story that is framed by someone else's lived experience. The journey we are walking together to rewrite the narrative of our stories begins by unpacking what you believe and why you believe it, and who has shaped the decisions you have made from this lived experience.

What do you believe about God?

Do you believe that your life has meaning and purpose?

What is beauty?

How does the impact of others perception of beauty change your story?

What is your relationship with authority?

Do you believe you have permission to make decisions about your own life's path?

A personal awakening happens when we allow the work to dig deep into the crevices of our stories. This process of awakening is the reframing of our pre-conceived bias about the people we encounter every single day. It is allowing space and time to reconcile what we believe about foundational building blocks of not only our worldview, but also where we get our sense of self.

Confidence in the power of my own story was built by knowing that the steps I was taking, albeit hard, were the right steps for me and my future.

I grew up thinking that I needed to get permission to live the story of my own life. I wanted to please my parents and those around me, not wanting to get anything wrong.

This seeking out of permission became a foundational stumbling block to discovering my own worldview and understanding of my own story.

I have found as I have talked to others about their stories, that often some of us can be hardwired to seek permission from others. As we grow up, we can be conditioned to ask someone else to validate every step we take.

Children need a parental figure to create boundaries for them as they grow and explore for safety. This is when seeking permission and sticking to the rules is important. There came a time though, when I needed to start taking responsibility for my own story and the decisions I was making. My children for example need me to say no for them, but there are times where I need to create an environment where they develop independence.

If we don't gain true independence from our family of origin stories, it can be hard for an adult to stop seeking permission. This gap in my story impacted the foundation of my identity and my understanding of where I belonged in the world.

Can I make my own decisions about God?

What if I believe something different to what my parents believed?

Who made up that rule in my life anyway?

Just like the monks as they arrived in the arid Australian outback and the indigenous landowners, the worldview that they both brought to those encounters shaped the decisions they made—harrowing decisions, painful decisions that created an earthquake of fear and misunderstanding.

We all have different stories and experiences when we try to communicate with one another, and we listen through the understanding we carry from our own culture and background. As we begin to write a new story, we can be stuck in an old story that is often written by our parents. I found this to be an opportunity to begin again. This new story is a co-creation with God and my own sense of direction, shaped and formed by my worldview.

I found that when I triangulated my sense of purpose by the validation of others I continually got stuck in my story. My mind was conditioned to seek permission from others. I learnt to unlock the greatest potential in my life, I needed to take hold of these old stories and rewrite them.

Here are four permissions I gave myself in this journey of discovery.

Firstly I gave myself permission to change. I realised that we are all in a state of becoming. No one is perfect and the art of maturing as we grow is to allow ourselves to change and become the deepest, most authentic versions of ourselves possible. I realised when I was always seeking permission from others to speak, invisible borders that were shaped by someone else's worldview surrounded me.

Secondly, I needed to permit myself to fail. The greatest critic we often face in this awakening of change is the way we speak to ourselves. As we explore change, listen to the way that you speak to yourself about failure. Often the greatest seasons of growth are found in the awakening of imperfection. You would never expect a toddler to run like an athlete, so be kind to yourself in this journey of discovery, and speak with a voice of compassion into your transformation.

Thirdly I needed to give myself permission to truly own my story. The part that we play in the burgeoning of self-awareness is pivotal. Self-reflection and the questions at the end of each chapter are an opportunity for you to field out the borders of your own story. Give yourself permission to be curious about where assumptions and themes in your story originated.

Lastly, I let myself laugh and have a little fun. As we go on this pilgrimage together, let's allow ourselves to have a little fun. Although the themes in this book are a little heavy, while they shine light into darkened places, we can also look at ourselves not too seriously. Let's find out little quirks about our own stories and personality that make us smile. You were birthed in beauty, joy and pain. Let's hold both the power of change and imperfection in both hands.

Discomfort is not always a bad thing. As we lean towards our difficult stories, there is an opportunity for change. Waking up to our story is the beginning of doing things differently.

Take some time now to reflect on these questions below. Brainstorm, write a letter or have a conversation with a friend about your story and your worldview. I have found in my life that permanent change comes when I apply what I am learning. Storytelling is a powerful tool for change because it helps us to apply the awakening of new information in our everyday.

What worldviews can you identify as coming from others?

When was the last time you realised you are changing?

What worldview do you hold that is different from your parents?

Do you feel afraid to speak from your own story? If so, what is holding you back?

Write Your New Identity Story

Old Story: I am not enough.
New Story: I am growing and changing every day.

Old Story:

New Story:

Bea

'You are imperfect, permanently and inevitably flawed. And you are beautiful.'

Amy Bloom

The role of physical beauty in our current culture is endemic. The media asks us to be more, to look a certain way and to change our understanding of what is beautiful. As women, our physical beauty impacts our work lives, relationships and opportunities.

Consistent messaging in the media and online about our worth and looks can impact every one of our stories each day. That feeling of not enough-ness impacts our identity in every single way. As we explore the impact of our upbringing and our understanding of identity, it is imperative that we unpack our understanding of beauty.

Amanda explores the impact of words, and the pack mentality of her ballet class, and Anne describes a regular story that sits on her therapist couch. This section of our book has the capacity to help you change your story on beauty and live awake to the way that God sees you.

Coming Home

Amanda Viviers

'It's a funny thing coming home. Nothing changes. Everything looks the same, feels the same, and even smells the same. You realise what's changed is you.'

F. Scott Fitzgerald

They whispered at the back of the bus, thinking I couldn't hear them. No matter how quietly someone whispers, we often know when a conversation is marked with gossip and our own name.

I was lying down trying to sleep as our troupe of dancers drove through the night to a festival many hours from our seaside town. The teenage girls giggled and snickered, one moment my teammates, then with three simple words, they tore my heart apart and became my enemy.

'Amanda, she smells.'

It wasn't just a childish, schoolyard taunt. It was a collection of mean words, making fun of something so very personal. As dancers, we were often sweating and dancing close alongside one another, and I listened there, in the dark of night, to words that penetrated deep into my heart and slashed my soul.

I was horrible.
I was repulsive.
I was dirty.
I was detestable.

Shame shattered my identity through those three little. I tried to shrink into a place where no one could see me. Saying to myself over and over, 'no one will ever love you, no one wants to be near you, you are repulsive'.

Three words, a group of girls laughing at the back of a bus, and my world shrank.

It took many years to reframe the story that carved itself on my heart that winter, as a fifteen-year-old girl. I wanted to escape the body that held my stories. I questioned whether anyone would ever love me. I believed them when their words told me my body would repel someone.

I was ugly and no one ever could love me.

These questions turned from a simply whispered taunt in the middle of the night into a raging eating disorder over a period of many years. Everything that happened across my teenage years made me want to escape the body my soul lived in. A body that always seemed to embarrass me. I decided very early on that my body could never be my home.

I wore a crocheted jade green jumper to my year twelve retreat. Once again I stepped onto a bus of teenagers. Fear gripped me as I walked through the throng of boys and girls. I heard a wolf whistle, I grimaced and turned back to see who was making fun of me. Escape, escape, everything in me wanted to escape. I was not safe in this body. It was not my home.

I am horrible.
I am repulsive.
I am dirty.

I am detestable.

Surely they are whispering about me. Maybe I can just sneak towards a seat and sit down. The guy who had wolf-whistled at me, walked along the bus aisle to find me.

'Amanda, you are beautiful'.

Four words that every teenager longed to hear from the class captain. Wasn't that the mecca of the high school experience?

Four words that I wanted to believe. Instead I said to him, 'Are you making fun of me?' He shook his head and walked away.

I heard him softly saying, 'The colour of your jumper matches the colour of your eyes'.

That encounter didn't make me stop losing weight by throwing up every meal. Instead, it propelled me further towards sacrificing myself so that others would compliment my external beauty. I wanted to be beautiful. I wanted someone to truly see me as beautiful. Even though I truly believed I was ugly.

If only I could lose more weight, then I would be more lovable.

My high school years were marked by these two opposite events on the school bus. It took many years to reframe these stories of my foundational truth of beauty. But until then I wanted to escape my body and the way it betrayed me so often. I was not comfortable in my own skin. It was my body that constantly reminded me of my shame. My body was not my home.

Most of us have stories about our bodies, and we have made our own meanings from those experiences. The result is the lived experience that we have creates the life we will live in the future. We cannot exist without our body and making peace with it, is one of the greatest gifts of coming home to ourselves.

I have never known a season or year that has passed across my whole life that my Mum or someone from my family has not been on a diet. I remember my dancing teacher pulling me aside, as an impressionable eleven-year-old, with a report from my dancing exam that said:

'Amanda has the potential to go all the way to the top as a dancer if she just lost weight.'

My teacher tried hard to shield me from the pain of that remark, written carelessly on such a formal piece of paper, but the wound slashed across my heart and I wrote the following on my soul;

Horrible.
Repulsive.
Dirty.
Detestable.

The power of words to shape our identity around the role of beauty in our lives is deeply formational. Words that people have spoken over our lives. Words that have been written down. And those that have been whispered on the back seats of buses, as we have shrunk into a corner trying desperately not to hear. I think we all hold a mirror inside our minds that questions whether we are beautiful enough.

There is a story from the beginning of time, where Eve stands in the garden, hiding from God because she knows something terrible has happened, and shame shrouds her soul. Heaven and earth were finished in the finest of detail. Before any grasses or shrubs were growing from the earth, God formed man out of the dirt from the ground and blew breath and life into his nostrils.

> *'The Man came alive- a living soul!'*
> *Genesis 2:7 (MSG)*

Then after this human walked the earth, the dirt, the clay, and the world for the first time, God planted a garden in Eden. Water started to flow throughout this land, and two trees shaped the purpose within the land—one for life and the other for good and evil.

> *'God made all kinds of trees grow from the ground,*
> *trees beautiful to look at and good to eat.'*
> *Genesis 2:8 (MSG)*

This is the first mention of the concept of beauty in the bible. The power of something physical that draws out a response in humanity, it is a moment of awakening. Beauty is designed to bring glory and joy as we look across the vista of creation. Just a few short verses later God said

> *'It is not good for man to be alone;*
> *I'll make him a helper.'*
> *Genesis 2:18 (MSG)*

It goes on to explain,

> *'The man and his wife, Eve, were naked,*
> *but they felt no shame.'*
> *Genesis 3:25 (MSG)*

These few short sentences in Genesis set the pre-cursor to the greatest wrestle in history. When shame entered the land and distorted our current view of beauty, the moment when everything changed. There was a shift in our understanding of what it means to be naked and unashamed, what is means to be beautiful and accepted just as we are. The result was generation after generation who have struggled with the external, versus internal, understanding of beauty. It impacts everything, especially our capacity to love.

> *'There is no fear in love. But perfect love drives out fear, because fear has to do with punishment. The one who fears is not made perfect in love. We love because he first loved us.'*
> *1 John 4:18-19 (NIV)*

Eve's body kept score and immediately she felt shame. She whispered to Adam that he needed to wear leather clothing to cover his naked body, and immediately they tried to hide from the presence of God. Something that was so natural and joy-filled, living free in the garden, walking with no shame, was now corrupted.

Recently I was a part of an exercise class that has helped me shift the role of shame in my body by helping me to breathe deeply into the places that I hold stress. I've been surprised at the beauty of deep breathing and how it has helped release old stories. It grounds us, reminding us that our body is a temple of the soul.

The teacher asked us to imagine somewhere in the world that we felt most at home, a place of comfort. I quickly scanned through some of my favourite places. The olive groves of Lebanon, the jungles of Thailand, the city where I lived and none of them made me feel like I was home. It wasn't the house I grew up in or the beach.

The place I felt most at home was with my family in my own lounge room because I felt safe. I cried and cried on the floor of that exercise class, because I realised I had been carrying so much pain and shame in my body, because I never felt safe in my own home. I imagined myself lying on the floor of my lounge room, releasing the shame my body had always carried. That feeling that I was not good enough and I was un-beautiful. They were old stories that needed to be rewritten into a new story. A story where I found love, acceptance and belonging.

I was at last home.

Coming home to my body through understanding my story, through journalling, counselling and reframing my worldview was an experience of healing across many decades. I made peace with the stories that have formed my self-perception and allowed myself to breathe deeply, with softness back into the beauty of my own body.

I think the most beautiful people in the world are not a size, shape or a particular colour, but those who have made peace within—those who have made their body not just a house but also a home.

Reflection

We all have stories of un-beauty that impact our story. These are the moments when we have not felt enough and wanted to hide in a corner somewhere. The power of writing and journalling to change your story is a powerful tool of transformation. The awakening comes from the way that we re-story. These questions are designed to help you reflect on your relationship with beauty and re-write the story.

What stories have impacted the way that you view your beauty?

If you could go back in time, what would you say to your younger self about her beauty?

Have you ever been bullied or heard someone say something mean about you?

Describe some of the ways you are beautiful inside and out.

Letting Go of Beauty

Anne

'To be beautiful means to be yourself. You don't need to be accepted by others. You need to accept yourself.'

Thich Nhat Hanh

The Old Story

When I first met 38-year-old Sunny, she was friendly and looked like she knew how to take care of herself. She was a part-time lawyer and told me she enjoyed her work. When I asked her if she had emotional support, she told me she had a kind partner, a good relationship with her two daughters, two sisters that would do anything for her, and a wide circle of friends; a few of whom she could speak to about anything. Sunny presented as a competent woman with the capacity for close relationships.

When I asked her what she wanted from therapy, she said that she had started to notice that both her daughters were talking badly about their bodies and that neither of the girls thought they were beautiful. They were always comparing themselves to their friends on Instagram. She said she thought it might be her fault and she didn't know how to fix them. She also told me that she goes to great lengths to affirm her girls inside and out.

My first thought was that it is not likely to be Sunny's fault. Sunny and her girls are living in a society that indoctrinates us all with untrue, sexist, and unrealistic standards of beauty ideals and 'perfect' female bodies. I thought that the best way to clean up her girl's self-narrative around beauty was to become curious about what views from society Sunny had taken on for herself.

Sunny started to tell me her childhood story. She told me about the large rammed-earth house on a hill; how her home was filled with laughter and storytelling, yummy dinners, new clothes, bike rides and adventures. Her parents were generous and often kind. Sunny had two sisters who loved her dearly, 'Well most of the time,' she said with a laugh. She told me that her mother spent a great deal of time talking with them, often gathered around the kitchen table. Sunny spent wonderful times with extended family and spoke of how loved she was by her grandparents, aunts and uncles. Well-liked, her family would regularly be invited to spend time with other families. She told me about friends she had in high school that she still caught up with on occasion. Sunny mentioned a few romantic relationships growing up that were nothing too serious until she met Chris. She described their relationship as a whirlwind romance that eventually became a stable base for their two children. She shared that her girls are full of fun and easy to be around. They both enjoy school. Sunny said she gets tired sometimes, but she copes alright. Her partner Chris has a good sense of humour, is responsible with the children and does an equal share of the household chores.

While I was holding in mind her desire to get her girls to stop speaking badly about their bodies, I was listening for evidence to validate or invalidate my guess that Sunny had taken on stories about how women are not good enough just the way they are. As Sunny began to trust me more, other stories unfolded.

One day in her ninth year, Sunny was sent to her neighbour to deliver a message from her mother. Within minutes the little girl ran back home, literally beaming from ear to ear, 'Mum, Mum, Uncle Bob said, 'Thanks Sunny, you're so beautiful!

He said I was beautiful!'

Her mother replied with a quizzical laugh, 'He didn't mean you looked beautiful, he meant it was lovely of you to run over the message.'

Crestfallen, Sunny began to reason. *Oh... Uncle Bob doesn't think that I actually look beautiful. How silly of me. Of course.*

It's doubtful that it was her mother's intention to give her a message of unbeauty, and yet, here is Sunny in the present moment narrating a tale from long ago as a moment where she decided she was unbeautiful.

When I asked Sunny why she thought it was silly to think the neighbour might mean she was beautiful, she said that it was her sisters who were the beautiful ones. When I invited her to give me an example of what she meant, she told a story of how she shared a bedroom with her sisters. Sunny told me that their two beds sat adjacent at one end of the room, and her bed sat alone at the other end. 'One time' she recalled, 'I remember standing between the beds where my two sisters lay asleep under their blankets. Just looking at the hand of my older sister on the edge of her mattress, with her perfectly shaped fingers with long, straight nails made me feel bad about my short, stumpy fingers. My sister's sun-kissed golden-brown, wavy hair was so thick that it seemed to cover the whole pillow, not like my limp, dull hair,' she said.

She turned to see her younger sister's form. 'She was different, but no less beautiful,' said Sunny. 'Gorgeous chocolate ringlets. You know, the kind that glide silkily around your finger. I could see her perfectly shaped leg sticking out from the sheet, unlike my tree-trunk legs. She had rosy cheeks and her face was just as perfectly proportioned as my other sister's. They both have even eyebrows and small, straight noses. Not like me. I have one eyebrow higher than the other and my nose is much too big for my face. My mother often commented on my sister's beautiful rosebud lips centred in smaller mouths, unlike my wide mouth that still attracts laughter when people view my baby photos.'

When Sunny had asked to have dental braces like her sisters, her mother responded, 'What for? Your mouth is big enough.' He mother meant that, unlike her sisters, there was enough room in her mouth for her teeth to straighten in their own time. Sadly, from that moment on, Sunny internalised her mother's voice to convey, I've got a big mouth, I'm too loud, why bother straightening my teeth, no point investing in ugly. Sunny told me how she couldn't help but feel jealous of her sisters and then hated herself for feeling that way.

As I sat adjacent to Sunny, my heart started to ache for her. She had been taught by this world that she needed to focus on hands, legs, hair, face, and all things pretty. Oh, Sunny, so deeply entrenched in her comparison story. And yet, I can honestly tell you that there was absolutely nothing wrong with her hands, her hair, her face, or anything else about her. Although I could not agree with the self-loathing I was hearing, I was keen to understand how these stories had influenced her current narrative.

With heartfelt sadness, I reflected to Sunny. 'It seems growing up you saw your sisters as beautiful and yourself as unbeautiful, and it makes sense to me now that you are worried that you have passed this unbeauty story onto your girls.'

'Yes, I think I've really screwed them up.'

'I think the world has screwed all women over with their beauty story, so I don't think this is about blame. It's more about the desire to understand and make positive change.

Unfortunately, Sunny had not detached from the world's story of beauty that says beauty is about being thin and having a symmetrical face. The Sunny's of this world, including myself at times, are constantly trying to live up to some imposed physical standard, and then using that standard to compare themselves with others. Sunny came to therapy to talk about her old story because she knew something was missing in how she was raising her girls. Sunny is looking for a new story, however, the TV and magazines messages will make her task challenging.

Sunny has lived out of a comparison relationship with beauty, which is what was addressed in our sessions. From a revised sense of self, Sunny found it easier to talk to her girls about what it is to be a woman in this world; to be respected and valued as a person.

Our stories will not evolve by themselves. Without reflection on the overpowering, relentless messages about how a women's worth is directly related to how they look, women will likely continue to live out of the dominant story society perpetuates.

The New Story

The new story is to reject society's unreasonable ideal of beauty. There are many ways to be beautiful. Society suggests physical beauty is some kind of unreachable ideal that no one seems to fulfil, but everyone has to work towards. That is not a message that God would be championing; His perfection is not a straight nose, it's multifaceted. Lack of self-acceptance and comparison to others leads to the search for one particular mark of idealised external beauty. Poisonous injections, and incisions made with surgical steel, can help to make some external changes, but if you are to believe in society´s values, you will never have enough beauty. You may have believed all your life that you have to be externally beautiful for someone to love you. But the truth is that this is not the only beauty that exists. Beauty can be defined as loving every part of you, despite what society tells you.

We have been sold a lie that beauty is one thing. But we can also think about beauty in a more useful way that lifts ourselves up. What if we think of it as something that evokes a delightful feeling in another? For example, while some women do have external beauty, some have olympic talent, others the ability to sing in a way that shakes us to the core, some help others with deep compassion, while others create beautiful things with their hands. The list could go on forever, but the message is the same: everyone has beautiful qualities, and no one is better than another for having that quality. The important thing is to comprehend beauty in its diverse and spectacular array.

My hope is that as Sunny gets to know the different parts of herself, even the parts she has been conditioned to loath, she will feel increasingly more beautiful. When we are feeling vulnerable by the self-stories we've taken on, it's so easy to believe what the world is telling us. A child lacks the capacity to challenge what is told to her over and over again by the world, even if the narrative is contested in the home. Sunny took on the 'lack of beauty' story and then believed it was her reality. The story became true at the very moment that she understood and believed that it was not a story, but her reality. It was only at that point that she started being unbeautiful in her own mind. Confusing a story with reality was not her fault. Childlike unawareness does not provide the opportunity to challenge the subliminal and blatant messages of beauty propaganda perpetuated by the ideals of modern society.

Let's take a look at how the therapy session continued as I encouraged Sunny to walk in a new story.

'Sunny, most women have defined their beauty based on an insane amount of sexist and elitist information that tells them as young girls that they have to look a certain way. The story your mother told you is the story that society had written for her. It's the same story that you are now holding for yourself.'

'Oh gosh, yes, I can hear myself being critical towards my own body. How do I stop that?' she asked.

'You can realise that just as you learnt that voice, you can unlearn it,' I said.

'Are you sure?' asked Sunny.

'Hard to believe, hey,' I replied.

'Yes. I don't think I can stop being critical, but maybe I can stop saying things out loud so my girls can hear,' said Sunny.

'Say things out loud?'

'Yeah, like saying that I need to lose weight to feel better about myself or complaining that I look old.'

That's a good strategy, but I'd love to see you walk in more freedom than that,' I said. Sunny looked sceptical but intrigued. I continued. 'The stories you say to yourself are just that, stories, man-made stories, not truths.'

Sunny looked at the floor in front of her, 'But the way I think about myself is the only story I know.'

'Yes, that's right Sunny. It is the only story that is upper-most in your mind, but an alternate story exists. Let's stop talking about a flawless, perfectly proportioned body as a benchmark for success, and let's start talking about you as a person.'

Unbeauty stories create wounds that will not heal on their own. What if, instead of attacking ourselves for things we did not choose or create, we could catch, contain and conceivably transform them.

There may have been positive beauty stories given to Sunny during her childhood, from her parents, her sisters, her grandparents, her aunts and friends. Yet Sunny's self-narrative was so firmly entrenched in what society deems beautiful that any stories she might have received about loving all the parts of herself would likely have been rejected or repressed. Long into adulthood, Sunny denied and excluded any information that did not fit in with her internalised definition of beauty. Until adult Sunny wakes up to revisit and reshape her old story, not much will change for her or her daughters.

I will try to help Sunny interrupt her unbeauty myths by saying things like 'when you hear that voice that focuses on physical beauty, tell it to LEAVE! Instead, say to yourself I'm working on a new story! Switch your focus onto something you feel passionate about, or something creative, or pursue a goal.'

Once Sunny learns to hear the unbeauty voice, she can catch it and rescript.

The first step to becoming awake to true beauty is the willingness to reject society's definition of beauty by reflecting on and questioning our long-held beliefs. When parts of the self are made redundant by a society that reduces a woman's worth to how she looks, it may seem impossible to think about the self in any way other than what is known and accepted. Especially when these views are also held by the people that matter to us.

True beauty is about moving from ideal to real, from fear to knowledge, and slavery to emancipation. Choosing to become awake and change your 'unbeauty' feelings about yourself can be difficult, especially when you are so deep in your unbeautiful story that you can't refute all the brainwashing stories that have been sold to you. Nonetheless, there are many ways to rewrite your beauty story.

Here are three practical ways to wake up to the truth that may live unacknowledged in the old story.

Imagine a New Way of Thinking

To people that don't like themselves much in general, it may seem like a fantasy to think of the self as beautiful by loving and accepting every part of the self. However, fantasy in the form of visualisation can be useful to help us make sense of an experience of which we have little knowledge. For example, we fantasise about our first day at high school or our first day at a new job, as a way of preparing ourselves for the occasion.

In the same way, begin to visualise yourself as beautiful in every way. Paint a picture in your mind of what true beauty and acceptance looks like to you.

Stop Placing the Emphasis on Bodies

When a mother constantly tells her girl that she looks pretty, in an attempt to push back against the tide of beauty propaganda, they are still purporting that their worth is connected to looking a certain way. Like praise for a good report encourages children to strive again to get that praise, similarly constant affirmations that you look pretty encourages girls to keep that focus. No matter how loud a mother shouts positive body image messages to her girls, it will never drown out the airbrushed photos seen on various media platforms. The quote below by Kasey is in the context of her heart-felt desire to take the emphasis off physical beauty.

'My goal is not for my girls to grow up feeling beautiful. Rather, it is for them to grow up not caring if they are or not.'

Kasey Edwards
Columnist and author of Raising Girls Who Like Themselves

The only way mums are ever going to give their girls a fighting chance of accepting their body and loving themselves is to stop placing the focus on their child's body. It is vital for mums (and dads) to stop commenting negatively on their child's body, their own body, and the bodies of other people. Even constant talk about being healthy can make a girl feel guilty for eating so much as a chocolate bar. If you want to talk about health, just say 'It's good to look after your body and all foods are good in moderation.'

Does that mean we want to silence body talk? No, of course not. We definitely want to tell our girls to love and appreciate their body. We can tell them that every part of their body is thoughtfully and beautifully designed by a God who loves how he made them. We just want to broaden our discussion about beauty. Sunny can influence her girls by concentrating conversation around things they have control over, such as the things they like doing or the way they do them. Children are naturally creative and curious. Place more focus on their personality and show interest in the things they take an interest in. In this way you are talking about the depth of beauty that God has made in us as far more than our bodies alone.

Prefer Acceptance to Comparison

I remember what a Year 7 teacher, Mr McNulty, once taught me about society's perpetration of comparison. 'I prefer not to teach kids self-esteem, which relies on comparison; instead, I try and teach them self-acceptance. '

Comparison encompasses more than just beauty. Our school years are often filled with comparison. For example, some parents can insist that their children are above average in some way, which completely disregards the bell curve that suggests only so many can be in the top 5%. In my time as a therapist within a school setting, the only parents happy with their child receiving an average academic mark were parents of children with learning difficulties. The message is clear; you are never enough, you have to be better than someone else to be 'someone', you have to be better than average. The emotional cost of this socially constructed, narrow message around comparison, including how people look, has led to a shattered understanding of beauty for many a teen.

The truth is that you are perfectly acceptable just as you are. You arrived in this world amidst awe and wonder, innocence and wisdom. Each person has a mixture of beautiful qualities. God does not seem to apologise for creating each woman uniquely beautiful. A confrontation between our beliefs about what is beautiful, and the reality of God's aesthetic concept may be needed to foster change. God has made you amazing, which is reflected in His perfection. Maybe it's time to accept the story you may not have heard, that YOU are unique and incredible. You are EXACTLY what God desired when he formed you in your mother's womb. And that society's definition of beauty is actually only a man-made construct.

It will require a certain amount of strength to reject the burden of the egregious, damaging, sexist, elitist, and entirely evil beauty stories you have heard all your life. It's time to let go of the wrong stories you have heard about beauty?

Leave your negative beauty stories where they belong - in the bin!

Reflection

Review these questions and see what old stories have come to the surface in your own life.

1. If you could go back in time, what would you want to say to your younger self about her beauty?

2. In what ways can you walk away from false beauty ideals?

3. What childhood memory do you have of your beauty? How do you think your relationship with TV, advertising and other forms of media have impacted your view of beauty?

4. Growing up, what parts of your physical looks were deemed unacceptable?

5. Growing up, what parts of your internal self were deemed unacceptable?

6. How many days can you go without talking negatively about your body?

7. What have you decided to see next time you look in the mirror?

Write Your New Beauty Story

Old Story: I am ugly.
New Story: I am worthy of love and belonging.

Old Story:

New Story:

Auth

'The essence of great leadership is influence not authority.'

Ken Lear

We each pick up an understanding of the role of authority in our lives from a young age. Whether it is a favourite teacher or an overtly strict parent, we can easily become stuck in the role of authority in our lives and where we get our permissions.

The greatest difficulty in regards to authority and living out our stories in the future is that we look for our permissions from these stories that hold us contained. If we have a healthy understanding of the role of authority and boundaries in our lives, we then thrive in the midst of change and transition.

However, if we have formed unhealthy relationships with authority in the past, fear can hold us in a locked pattern trying to gain the attention and permission from anyone around us. Growing in our self-authority understands our boundaries and where our permissions lay.

Across this section of the book, Anne and Amanda talk about stories from both their childhood and adulthood to unpack the rewriting of the story of authority and its role in their future stories. This powerful discussion about the ways that we can be both submitted and full of courage to find our voice in the workplace and our family homes is an opportunity for new conversations around leadership in the future.

Holding the Key

Amanda

'When we fail to set boundaries and hold people accountable, we feel used and mistreated.'

Brené Brown

I sat on my boss's couch, eight months pregnant, and a tear dripped down my face without a word even being spoken. The fear that rippled through our offices that day was hanging around like a fog, produced by the whispers behind closed doors. Hour upon the hour, some of my closest friends sitting on that same couch, were released from the leadership roles we held in the congregation.

Redundant.
Meaning we have no use or purpose for you any longer.
Superfluous.

The whole team was made redundant in one day. It was a complete shock to us all. There was no season of transition or conversation. That was the hardest part of this experience. We had just walked through a season of deep grieving, and we were bound together by the trust it had built.

Then, in a moment, there was a brutal severance that was deeply formational in my understanding of what it felt to be betrayed by the church.

They said.

'This is God's plan.'

I heard *'God doesn't need you any longer, used and thrown away.'*

'We've been praying and the season has now passed.'

I interpreted, *'I'm no longer valid or have a place in leadership.'*

'It's time to do the best for the congregation.'

My voice said, *'Even though we have sacrificed all for that congregation, I no longer belong.'*

Often the words that are spoken in times of radical change can be the most painful because they are shrouded in justification and defence. That moment when I was released from a leadership team I had walked with for over a decade, was one of the saddest days of my life.

It wasn't the role. I was offered many new roles in the coming few months. It was how the transition was handled, the manipulation, and the betrayal from conversations that were held in secret. This subversive culture within teams creates an epidemic of mistrust, and it is very difficult to restore the deep wounds it creates in a community of people.

The role that authority plays in our lives is an interesting one. There is an important part that it plays in creating safe and flowing communities, but at the same time, what happens when this relationship is unsafe?

Our experience of authority will determine our capacity to relate to authority. Proper authority involves respect. It is not imposed from on high. It is a shared understanding that transcends power imbalance to include mutual benefit and respect.

What people think of their boss may sometimes mirror how they see parental authority.

- My boss doesn't look after me.
- My boss frightens me.
- My boss personalised criticism.
- My boss won't talk to me.
- My boss over-exercises authority.

Consistent experiences with authority that was too severe may impair our ability to hold appropriate authority in the world. We may become either too bold or too timid.

My husband did something really brave that week as I sat at home with what should have been a time of rest before my first child was born. Instead, I was grieving the pain of the way this transition was employed. He went to the most expensive street in our city, found Tiffany's, and bought me a new necklace. He did this to congratulate me on my retirement from work for a season!

I laughed out loud with him. Retired at thirty-six, I am living the dream!

The most beautiful part of this gift he bought me is that the necklace held on its thread a big silver key. He looked at me with compassion and said, 'My dear, this is just the beginning, this season of motherhood will unlock many new paths in your life. The role you held, even though it has shaped and formed so much of your identity, that role is not who you are. You are so much more.'

Permission to change.
Permission to grieve.
Permission granted to hope again.

My faith in Jesus has been a massive part of this rediscovering the power of authority in a good way. Although I struggled with that story of redundancy, I began to learn once again the power of Jesus rewriting a new story from this old story that wanted to hold me captive. An awakening of permission, understanding that I had authority through Jesus to step into the purpose and potential that he had for my life.

The power of this gift of relationship through Jesus Christ unlocked doors that were seemingly closed. That's what I love about God, he sent his Son to earth to rewrite our stories through forgiveness and hope.

The doors that man tries to close, God will reopen in new ways. That is the power of the gospel. That is the beautiful finishing work of the authority of Christ and his exchange made at the cross.

One man reaching across history, to finish the work of the Father with a quiet whisper;

He came into the depths of the earth and stole back the keys of heaven, allowing us to live in full freedom with God, the Father.

He shouted.

'It is finished'.

Finished for our sake.
Finished by complete mercy.
Finished by Jesus.
Finished for you.

His finishing work on the cross is the key that unlocked my permission to live a life of freedom and liberty. Permission to truly become everything I was designed to become.

This is true freedom. To understand our personal authority in Jesus Christ becomes a powerful tool to rewrite the redemptive story we were always designed to live in. I realised I got so much of my sense of self, from what I did, the role that I held, a position of power, that I needed to reframe where I got my sense of worth from.

When I thought my work and reputation was forever to be made redundant and of no worth, my husband modelled this beautiful redemptive step of love modelled by his own relationship with Christ; in the way he walked me with kindness through this season. We are worthy, no matter the role we carry in an organisation or community. We are important, whether we carry the title of leader or not. So often I found my confidence waning in this season, because I didn't have a role to hide behind.

Over the next few months as I walked out the journey of novice motherhood, and the grief of losing a relationship with something I held so dear in my heart, over and over I was given keys from many different people in seemingly random sets of circumstances.

The message was coming through loud and clear, that this shift was not the end of my story; it was just a season of recovery from loss. It was a hidden season of rewriting an old narrative, especially the one I got from my identity from a role and a title. I went through a season where I needed to reframe where I got my permission from in authority and whether a job description on a paper made me a leader, or was it a calling that would continually lead me home.

Reflection

We all have very different relationships with authority. Our understanding of leadership and the way that we react to positions of authority, are always interweaved with stories from our past. Stories when our trust has been betrayed, when we have been told things that suppresses our voices, when we were forgotten and left aside. Your relationship with authority and the permission you give yourself to live with freedom stems from these narratives written on our hearts.

Take the time now to reflect on your own relationship with authority.
What story shaped your relationship with authority?

When have you felt unheard by authority?

Have you ever felt rejected by those in authority? If so, what can you learn from this?

When have you found yourself floundering from decisions made by someone else?

What authority do you need to take in your own life?

*'Your power to choose can never be taken from you.
It can be neglected, and it can be ignored. But if used,
it can make all the difference.'*

Steve Goodier

I was around 37 years old when I came home to self-authority. I had been working on my final assignment for most of the day. It was around 7 pm when I took a break to have dinner. I was bragging to my family over the evening meal that this was the last time I was ever going to be chained to a desk for an entire weekend. They were happy for me that my studies were at last coming to an end.

Swallowing the last bite, I returned to my computer to put the finishing touches on my work. Oh no! My computer wouldn't turn on. Random program corruption errors and frequent crashes over the past few months had warned me that my laptop might be dying a slow death, but I was hoping it would stay with me until I finished my degree and had the money to pay for a new one. But my computer was dead, and my assignment was gone. Just when I was so close to the finish line. I began to cry.

Normally I would have collapsed in a heap, felt like the world was against me and phoned a friend. Then something incredibly weird happened. I realised that I didn't have the urge to reach out to someone, to tell someone what happened, to get help or comfort from anyone else. I didn't feel alone or needy. I had this strange feeling of being accompanied. It was like I had a trustworthy parent with me; an internalised locus of security. I can only describe it as similar to a memory of being a little child leaning against my father's chest. His baritone voice would echo into me, making me feel like I was protected. For the first time in my life, I recognised myself as mature enough to manage this experience by myself. In some way, before that moment, I was still a little girl who needed my husband, someone else, or God, to calm me down.

In that moment, I had the pleasure of being able to observe my thoughts, contain my feelings, and reason a way forward. All the strengths I had absorbed from my parents and my own life experiences showed up and I was able to parent myself. My inner child was hurt and upset, but my adult self had the ability to be there for her. Even though I'd been fully grown for many years, I finally had the experience of being an adult! I felt like it was all going to be ok. I was strong, capable, and able to trust myself to work it out. I wiped my tears, grabbed my hubby's computer and within minutes started again. I held authority over myself.

From this moment of being there for myself, I have been aware of how liberating it is to have self-authority. Awakening to self-authority looks different for each person. For me it was a shift in self-talk. Instead of telling myself that I needed someone else to help me I told myself that I can take care of the little hurt girl inside. My claim to self-authority left me feeling less needy and this feeling permeated my whole life. Before this awakening, I realised that parts of me unconsciously objected to caring for myself because I often had to care for myself while growing up. Since waking up to self-authority, I've been better able to support myself and make decisions with confidence. Other people's opinions about me matter less because I don't rely on their input or approval anymore.

'Speaking from your original self (the author)
gives you natural authority.'

Lou Solomon

Authority is a Birthright

Authority is given to us at birth and is held by our parents until we are of a conscionable age to make our own decisions. There comes a time when a child is old enough to distinguish itself from others and can understand the difference between its own internal world and external reality. If there are any developmental hiccups in this kind of perception, it affects our confidence in our own authority. I regularly hear clients say things like, 'I'm not sure if I'm reading the situation correctly,' or 'I'm too afraid to decide in case I make a mistake,' or 'Can you please tell me what's the right thing to do in this situation?' These questions are unconscious requests for authority. If we don't author our own stories, we leave a door open for others to jump in and tell us how to live.

Don't give away your authority. Define yourself before someone else does.

Think of Rapunzel in her tower waiting for a prince to save her when she could have just cut off her own hair and used it as a rope to save herself. Don't wait for others to look after or define you. Naturally it can raise feelings of discomfort and anxiety when we want to clarify a new position in an old story. However, let me remind you that you can change your story. The key is to realise that your story is not fixed, but flexible.

A memory is something fixed;
like the way Grandma's apple pie tasted.
A story is much more flexible; like changing your mind.

Becoming Self-directed

Successfully taking over the job of self-authority from our caregivers is known as individuation, which is a developmental process wherein we realise we are a separate person to others and embrace our uniqueness. It is reaching a point where we can say, this is where you finish, and here is where I start. We begin to establish our own boundaries as we integrate all that has happened to us; the experiences we've had of our parents, friends, teachers and the world. The progression of individuation can be quite challenging for parents. They teach us what to think, feel and how to be in this world. Parents know that their child needs to become their own person and yet they expect their child to respond in the way that they always have. Parents don't often see the individuating process as refreshing independence. It usually ruffles a few feathers when their child no longer fits neatly into the parent's mould. Even though we reach adulthood, it can be a common response to feel 14 years old again when our parents correct us. Some children grow up to be adults who cannot tolerate the tension individuation presents, and will likely have life-long trouble saying *no* to their parents.

The extension of individuation comes later in life, and this is called differentiation. There are many existing interpretations of differentiation around. I think about differentiation as a continuum stretching from over-connected, where you are enmeshed in your relationships with others, to completely disconnected, where you are totally separated from others. Well-differentiated people are neither totally dependent on others nor completely independent; they are interdependent.

Differentiated people stay away from extremes and are considered to be closer to interconnected on the continuum. Some people move countries to get away from toxic people, or even leave marriages to be self-determining, which in some cases is necessary to keep yourself safe. However, out of sight, out of mind, doesn't necessarily mean that they are unconstrained. Some people remain influenced by others even though there is no more contact. They are still not free to live in their own self-authority. Their old story still influences their choices and behaviours, even though the other is no longer present. To have authority over ourselves, we need to be separate enough so that other people cannot determine our inner state and be connected enough to tolerate difference.

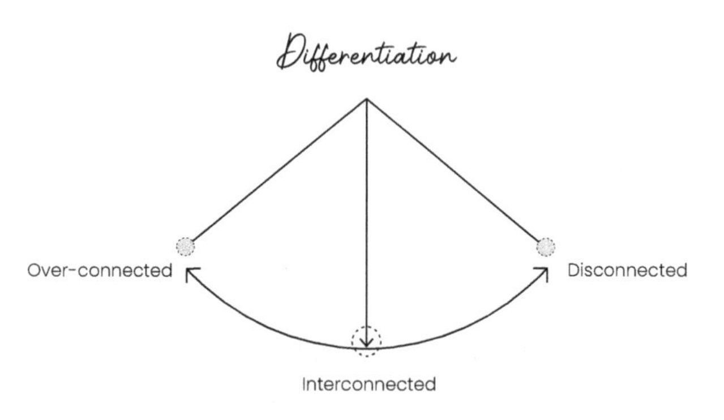

Let me give you a simple example of differentiation from my own relationship. A while ago, I had a few people over for afternoon tea. My husband was at work during that time, and returned about an hour after everyone had left to find that I was upset. Several very deep scrapes had been made by a toy right across my recently laid, very expensive, wood floors. They were ruined!

My husband responded, 'They're just floors. I like the lived-in look anyway. Don't worry about a few scrapes.'

I replied, 'It's okay that you feel differently than I do about the floors. But I need you to care that I'm upset - even if you disagree with me.'

He hugged me, and we went on to talk about what to have for dinner.

My undifferentiated self would have been mad as hell at his initial response. I would have wanted him to think and feel exactly the same way I did. And if he didn't agree with me, then I would have emotionally cut him off for the night while licking my wounds. I would have felt lonely and totally disconnected from him. However, I was more in my differentiated self at that moment, and this event didn't spoil our whole evening. I was able to hold onto my opinion while remaining emotionally connected to my husband. I told myself that it was okay for him to have a different opinion, and also reminded him that it was equally okay for me to think and feel differently. We managed to stay connected while having separate feelings about the issue at hand. I was able to hold my self-authority while respecting his.

Of course, it's still a journey to live out self-authority even when you become awakened. Here is an example where I demonstrated a lack of self-authority. I was in the dentist chair and I needed two fillings, one on either side of my mouth. My face began to lose feeling, and I found I could no longer open my mouth. Claustrophobic feelings arose in me as I couldn't take a breath. I focussed on breathing through my nose and mentally calming myself to get through it. I found out later that the dentist should never have numbed both sides of my mouth at the same time. But when it was happening, did I say, 'Help, I can't breathe. Something's wrong'? Nope. Not a word to him. I was listening to my internalised parent voice that says, *don't make waves*.

You may have experienced the opposite internalised parent voice that says, *speak up strongly* about every little thing. Children that have experienced too much harsh authority can result in adults that are very judgemental with themselves, and perhaps with others too. They may be prone to unrelenting standards that place excessive emphasis on rigid rules and ways of being in this world. This parenting style results in a lot of should's... *I should go to the gym* even though I'm exhausted; *you should fold the washing this way*. If parents were abusive, adult survivors can either over-exercise authority or become so frightened of becoming like their abusive parent that they cut off their authority and become too timid.

Authority over Thoughts and Emotions

Only when I take careful notice of whatever emotion I am rousing and the thoughts that accompany it, can I be awake to self-authority. Our thoughts and feelings work together so instinctively that if we don't intentionally reflect on what's happening inside ourselves, we're left with a limited ability to inhibit a response that is not mutually respectful. This is such a subjective process. However, if we never examine what drives us, we will likely end up at unintended destinations. Often people don't give attention to separating out their thoughts and feelings. A tip I give clients is: if you're using more than one word you are generally describing a thought. Use one word to tell me how you feel.

Developmentally, we learn how to control our feelings quite early in life, whereas the ability to reflect develops much later. This explains why adolescents can have such a hard time thinking before they act. How many times have I been in my impulsive teenage self, and gone from 1-10 in an instant? I know that I walk in greater self-authority when I can speak my mind gently, to myself and others. If I'm not in gentle authority, I can be quite harsh with others when I set a boundary.

Or conversely, I might avoid setting a boundary if I lack self-authority. However, I can only do that when I at least have some control over my thoughts and feelings. Waking up to self-authority means waking up to our thoughts and feelings which enables us to speak up for our needs.

Thoughts and Feelings

We might not recognise that authority is ours to claim, especially if we weren't encouraged to push back on authoritative ideas throughout our teen years. I often ask young adults with symptoms of anxiety: 'Do you have opinions that your parents wouldn't agree with?' Challenging adopted thoughts about values and rules to see if we want to keep them, allows us to develop our own self-authority. It's empowering to be able to express opinions with confidence.

No-one is the owner of truth.

We speak to ourselves and others as though our language has a shared meaning. However, how many times do we get upset with others when they don't think in a way that seems so simple and obvious to us?

I often ask couples, 'Is it ok for your partner to think differently to you?'

'Of course!' they exclaim.

I reply, 'You both say yes, but when it comes down to it, you really want the other person to agree with you, right?'.

This comment always brings a smile because there is a truth to it that we don't really recognise. It can be a tough gig to allow others to think differently from us, but when we make space for difference, we can walk in self-authority while also respecting the self-authority of others.

The trouble is that often, as soon as we want to speak up about something that is important to us, we have to start dealing with big emotions. Emotions are a reflection of the meaning and importance of whatever we experience. Emotions can help us take up authority by informing us, but not by running the show. We will need to reflect on, and contain, whatever feelings we experience from our emotional reactions in order to establish self-authority.

Self-authority is traceable back to emotional provocation. When I recognise my feelings as my own and examine them, I am in my best self. When I falsely identify my feelings as a result of someone else, I am in trouble because I have given them authority over me. One cannot deny that other people's actions influence us feel to certain ways. We can't control their actions, but we can increase our awareness about what we feel after those actions. When we discover our ability to identify and regulate our emotions no matter what other people do, then we are starting to gain authority over our self.

Speak up for Your Needs

When we lack self-authority, we lack power. When we lack power, we may claim it roughly from others. This might be from the underlying anger of not speaking up for what we need, or perhaps from having very little experience in speaking up. You most probably have stories of when your parents didn't have the capacity to absorb the perspectives of others. If this happened regularly enough then you probably won't exercise authority well. Because people who lack the capacity for self-authority cannot yet imagine having it, they rarely complain about its absence. They just want to feel more confident. When you're nurtured by competent parents, you are more likely to access authority early, consistently and respectfully.

Often, we speak when we shouldn't and don't speak when we should. Literature suggests that women can be inclined to make greater progress in assertiveness when they are pregnant. Somehow protecting a baby increases assertiveness. Typically, people don't speak up when they are annoyed about something because they have not been shown how to speak up well. They have been taught that when angry, they should either shut up or yell. They haven't been educated to occupy a more middle ground and say their piece gently.

If you think it feels right to say, err on the side of speaking up. Yet how do you know when to speak and when to keep quiet? This is where it's good to know yourself. For me, when I have a lump in my throat - there is something on my heart to say. If I have a sense of being rebellious - I know not to speak. If you are in your right space of legitimate authority, you will be self-disciplined enough to listen to the little voice inside you. You will know when to be brave, and you will have the courage to speak. You will also know when to keep your thoughts to yourself. If you are right to speak, it will channel something helpful. If you are not right to speak, it will be empty – like gossip or harsh criticism. It fills no one and nothing. It simply leaves us with a hollow, empty feeling.

Acknowledging responsibility for thoughts and emotional experiences is a difficult but rewarding process that leads to self-direction. It's time to live in your new authority story.

Reflection

What follows is a series of ideas and questions that can help you identify your relationship with authority and self-authority. Try answering the questions as honestly as possible and reflect on your answers.

1. Conscious living is true self-authority. When are you faced with an opportunity to make a decision, from whom do you seek approval?

2. On a scale of 1 to 10, how often are you able to be mindful of your thoughts and feelings?

3. Imagine you are in a meeting, and you want to speak about something that concerns you, but you are hesitant. Ask yourself this:

    - Do I believe my thoughts and opinions have value and deserve to be heard?

    - How do you feel about voicing your own opinions and concerns?

    - What stops you from owning your opinions?

4. We often don't know what the right thing is to do or to say. Next time this happens, try this exercise and fill in the blanks:

I am thinking ____

____

____

I am feeling ____

____

____

I desire/need ____

____

____

Therefore, it feels right for me to say/do is ________________________

____

____

Write Your New Self-Authority Story

Old Story: I have nothing to say.
New Story: I am worth listening to.

Old Story:

New Story:

Self

Comp

'Awakening self compassion is often the greatest challenge people face on the spiritual path'

Tara Brach

The greatest act of rewriting our future happens when we change the way we speak internally to ourselves. Self-compassion is an exercise in kindness and humility, as we give ourselves the same language of love and compassion that we extend to others.

In this section of Awake, Anne and Amanda take you through the challenges they have experienced in re-authoring their stories of self-compassion. When we change the way that we see our own stories through the lens of compassion, everything changes.

The places where we are stuck begin to change and we live in our new stories.

Every one of us is a walking catalogue of helpful and unhelpful narratives. We can be so deep in these archives that it's hard to unravel the yarns. We promise ourselves that something will change, but year after year, we walk the same, familiar path.

Self-compassion is the healer that changes our story.

Awake to Self-Compassion

Anne

'If your compassion does not include yourself it is incomplete.'

Jack Kornfield

Amy arrived at work before 8 am and opened her laptop to find Brogan's email.

> *Dear Amy*
> *Can we catch up for a chat today at 4 pm? If this isn't convenient, please let me know.*
> *Brogan*

Amy's mind was racing. Did I say something wrong to someone? Am I being retrenched like Cam last week? Did I stuff up the Robinson report?

Amy couldn't focus. Her worry started to turn to anger. Why did her boss want to see her anyway? Surely, it's good manners to let someone know why you want to speak with them in the first place. She returned his email.

> *Hi Brogan*
> *4 pm, no problem. Can you tell me what we'll be discussing so I can be prepared?*
> *Thanks,*
> *Amy.*

She began watching the clock. 10 am. 11 am. 12 pm. No response from Brogan. Dread began to invade her body. This is not a new story for Amy. Whenever Amy feels extreme self-disappointment or fear, she finds it almost impossible to calm herself down. This old story is rooted in early family experiences. During childhood, Amy was taught that she could not afford to make a mistake. When Amy made a mistake, her father would rant endlessly, sometimes bringing up her error again and again for days at a time. This was so painful for Amy that she tried super hard not to make a mistake, so she didn't have to feel this sting.

As Amy sat in the lunchroom and tried to figure out what she was in trouble for, her thoughts drifted to past mistakes: sending the quarterly report with a few spelling errors; lumping a whole pile of receipts together instead of putting them through one at a time; getting off early every Thursday to take Michael to footy training... Amy was becoming more and more upset. She thought about the job she didn't apply for last year because she didn't think she was good enough. Amy's distress peaked when she looked back to three weeks ago. She had stayed back at work and was late picking up Michael from the shopping centre. The 13-year-old was left alone in the dark carpark for almost half an hour. The image of his worried little face came to her mind.

No longer able to eat her lunch, Amy decided to pack up her things and go for a walk. Taking the stairs too quickly, Amy experienced a sharp tightness in her chest. Her heart was pounding. She couldn't touch on her surroundings, time seemed both fast and slow and she couldn't tell which step went up and which one went down. Unable to get a full breath, she collapsed against the rail, head spinning. There was no one to hear her cry for help. She was frightened. Amy thought she was going to die. Squatting on the step, unable to move, Amy had no choice but to lean on the wall and wait. After a little while, her breath became more even and she found the strength to climb the stairwell back toward her office. She did not tell anyone about what had happened.

Sweaty and restless, Amy managed to stay at her desk fidgeting with different tasks while ruminating on the possible scenarios she would soon face. Finally, at 4pm, she sat opposite Brogan, who was distracted enough that he didn't notice Amy was rattled.

'Thanks for popping in Amy. I just wanted to be the first to let you know we landed the Robinson account. Couldn't have done it without your report...'

Amy was so convinced she was in trouble that the relief was palpable.

'Are you okay?' asked Brogan.

'Yes, absolutely. I'm just relieved that I'm not in trouble.'

'Why would you be in trouble?' he asked.

'No reason,' she replied.

It was a good question, thought Amy.

Later that evening, Amy arrived in Dr Campbell's office with her heart still banging in her chest. She told him that she was worried because earlier she couldn't breathe and felt like she was going to die. Dr Campbell assessed her and diagnosed a panic attack. After an in-depth conversation, Dr Campbell asked, 'Do you often beat yourself up over mistakes?'

Um, I guess so,' said Amy.

Dr Campbell handed Amy a pamphlet and offered a suggestion, 'I know a local person who runs a group you might want to take a look at.'

Amy knew she had to do something. She didn't want to feel that frightened ever again. She read the blurb on how the group supports people to grow in self-compassion.

Mindfulness Compassion Group
Learn to develop a self-compassionate heart

Taking one of the empty seats, Amy had second thoughts. This group wouldn't solve anything.

The facilitator, Jill, had kind eyes and welcomed her to the group. Amy was feeling very uncomfortable but felt she had to stay now, at least for one session. Within minutes all the seats were taken.

For the benefit of the newcomers, Jill explained some of the rules around confidentiality and respectful turn-taking. She clarified that the group is not a formal program as such, however, she might add in a teaching moment here and there. Generally the group tended to learn from each other's experiences.

'We can all get stuck in one point of view. Basically, my job is to help each of you shift your attention toward accepting alternate views, in particular, the view from your compassionate self. Don't worry if you can't find your compassionate self at first. We're all here to help you find it.' Jill takes a pause to let her words sink in. 'To begin with, I'll ask who'd like to share an experience, and together we'll look for the compassionate self in that experience.'

'What is compassion? Would anyone like to talk about how compassion has helped them?'

Donna works in HR and has been a part of the group for seven months now.

Donna said, 'When people are angry about what has happened to them in the workplace, I tend to lean into what they're saying rather than pulling back.'

Jill reflected, 'So you see anger as a kind of suffering and are less afraid of people's suffering. That's awesome, Donna. Can you let the group know why you lean in instead of pulling back?'

'Yes. I'm listening for any ways that I can help them,' said Donna.

'Perfect. Yes, that's our explanation for this group. We use Paul Gilbert's definition that says, 'Compassion is a sensitivity to suffering in self and others with a commitment to try to alleviate and prevent it[2].'

Amy starts to feel a little more settled as she listens to Jill, and likes the idea of alleviating suffering but she's not sure how. She is drawn back to Jill's voice...

'We want to help you develop a part of the self that is compassionate. Then that compassionate self can turn towards the part of the self that is struggling. So, compassion is more than just kindness and understanding, it's a willingness to act on that feeling by doing something to relieve the suffering. When we enter the group, we give permission to others to lean into our suffering.'

Amy suddenly thought that she didn't want random strangers leaning into her in any way. She could barely talk to herself about how awful she felt, and she didn't know anyone here. Jill happened to cut across her thoughts in just the right moment.

'Always remember that we also have the choice to say 'I want to share, but I don't want any feedback.'

Amy smiled to herself. Maybe Jill was prophetic!

Jill continues, 'I know there are times when I can't find my compassionate self. It's like when I play a game of 'find the lolly' with my grandchildren. I hide a lolly in my left hand and show my empty right hand. My grandie looks for the lolly, and I say, Gone, like I have no idea where it went. Sometimes I'm like that puzzled child, certain my compassionate self has disappeared into thin air. It's just gone!' The group shared a laugh at Jill's tone of voice.

Jill seems real and normal enough to Amy. Amy likes how Jill seems to explain things simply.

'Let's take a moment to bring our mindful self into awareness,' Jill said. 'Close your eyes and start by focussing on your breathing. If you don't want to close your eyes, you can look down at the floor and find a spot to focus.'

Amy felt a little self-conscious, but she closed her eyes. Her senses became heightened. She hears people shift in their chairs.

'Slow down your breath by taking a long, even breath in and a long, even breath out,' Jill said. 'Enjoy the feeling of control. Enjoy the feeling of choice. Decide how long to breathe in and how long to breathe out.'

Jill is silent as she gives the group a few moments to sink into the exercise.

'Now we're going to bring to mind a place where we feel safe. It can be a real or imagined place. Some people might not know what a safe place looks like to them because it's not something that comes readily to mind. That's ok. Give it a go.' Jill waits a minute for the group to get there.

'Anyone not yet in a safe place, raise your hand if you need more time.' One hand peeks up. 'If you can't think of one, it is okay to use my safe place. Imagine sitting under a big oak tree, in a massive field with no-one around. You're sitting on a bench under your tree, and the branches are hanging down around you. Almost like the branches are protecting you from the outside world.'

Amy is not really focussing on what Jill is saying. She sees herself walking along the beach on the warm, soft sand.

'Now let's imagine ourselves filling up with compassion; a warm, golden glow that gently brings light to the whole inside of your body and you feel softer everywhere. Look for any tension in your body and let compassion wash over those tense places.

Amy scans her body from her head to her toe. She notices tension in her stomach and try's Jill's suggestion to let the warm golden glow and kindness soften and wash over the tension she is holding in her stomach. Amy feels the tension release a little. She becomes aware again of Jill speaking...

'...allow a smile to come to your face, think about a person, a pet, someone that cares about you, maybe even someone in this group. Allow the feeling of warmth and kindness to spread through your body. You may feel some resistance coming up or a block to feeling the compassion. Imagine yourself interested and motivated to help the resistance. Ask the resistance why it won't let compassion in. What does the resistance say to you?'

Amy notices that it's hard to let her stomach relax completely.

Jill continues, 'Maybe the resistance is saying 'shame.' Perhaps you think you don't deserve compassion, which rationally you know is crazy because everyone deserves compassion.'

'Maybe the resistance is saying 'weakness'. Perhaps you still think being compassionate to yourself is a weakness or you're just too tired to be compassionate to yourself.'

'Whatever the resistance is for you, let the resistance know that you accept it and lean in with love and understanding toward the resistance,' Jill said.

The minute Jill spoke the word 'shame', Amy knew instinctively that it was shame for making mistakes that was sitting in her tummy. Without thinking, Amy just let the warm glow of compassion melt into that shame feeling in her tummy. She began to feel tears well and was immediately thankful that she and everyone else had their eyes closed.

Jill invited the group to be present with each other.

'Let's wiggle our toes and bring our attention back to the group. Gently open your eyes when you're ready. You may want to bring up the resistance you just felt or something that happened to you this week. Who would like to begin?'

To the outside world, Maddy's husband was the perfect gentleman. She was certain that no court would believe her testimony. There were no faded bruises for evidence. He would get equal access to the kids, and she would not be there to stop from him telling James that he was a stupid boy. There would be no one to stand in the way of him yelling at Katie one inch from her face. Maddy mostly worried that he might make good on his threat to tell the courts she is a bad mum and take the kids full-time.

Maddy began.

'I hate looking in the mirror. I just see the same person. How long have I been coming here and telling you that I'm going to leave him and get the kids out? And another week's gone by, and nothing's changed. I'm still the same gutless person I was eight months ago.'

Amy's heart went out to Maddy. She couldn't believe that Maddy thought this about herself. When Amy had shown up tonight, Maddy was the only one who had silently welcomed her with a big smile. We can see in Maddy's example how we can be super harsh to ourselves and completely ignore the wonderful parts, in this case, Amy had felt welcomed by a friendly Maddy and so thought quite positively of her.

Jill said, 'So Maddy, you feel like you've let us all down. As though seven people are here waiting for you to share the news that you've left your husband?

Maddy replied, 'I'm not sure, yeah maybe.' Maddy's tears asked the group for space. And they gave it to her.

'Anyone have some thoughts? Can we move toward Maddy with compassion?'

Joan was the first to chime in. 'I would feel just as scared Maddy. We are all here for you however long it takes.'

In that moment Joan demonstrated 'shared humanity' where we can show compassion because, as humans, we share a common experience.

Keith said, 'I think you're doing your best Maddy.'

Amy could tell that the group felt warm towards Maddy. No-one seemed to be judging her.

Jill said, 'Can I offer a comment about what happened for me just then when you spoke?'

'Yes,' said Maddy.

'Maddy, when you said the word 'gutless,' it felt a little harsh to me. Did it feel a little harsh to you?'

Maddy nodded and maintained eye contact, so Jill continued.

'I had a kind of ouch feeling come up inside my body. Can we try the same sentence again with a softer, less critical tone in your voice? And maybe use a different word for gutless?

Maddy thinks for a moment. 'Um, I'm still too scared to leave, even with the support I've had from this group.'

Jill said, 'Wow Maddy, that's so powerful. I'm not sure you could have turned that last statement around so easily eight months ago. You've tapped into your compassionate wisdom.'

'Mm's,' and 'yeses' echoed around the group.

'That's right,' Keith added, 'When you said gutless, I thought that was pretty mean to yourself, but when you said you were scared it felt, um, softer, and definitely more compassionate and real.'

'Yeah I do feel less hard on myself. Less mean, when I say it differently,' agreed Maddy.

Jill nodded appreciatively at both Maddy and Keith.

'Thanks, Maddy. Keep practising your compassionate self-talk, and we will help you here in any way we can.'

Jill addressed the group. 'When our brains tell us we are in danger, it is hard to find our compassionate voice, mostly because we think we have to stay strong, or we might fall apart or lose control if we are kinder to ourselves. But what we find is that there can be much more strength in being compassionate.'

Amy wondered if her brain was telling her she was in danger on the staircase at work. She made a mental note to figure out what the danger was.

'Who else would like to share tonight?' Jill offered.

Dean said, 'I'll go next.' All eyes turned to Dean.

'Struggling this week to keep off the drink. To be honest, one of the things that kept me going was knowing I was coming tonight.'

Amy could feel the group give Dean their full attention. She wondered if this is what Jill meant about leaning in to suffering.'

Dean continued. 'Monday I was really thinking about taking a drink, y'know? And to be honest, I drove up to the bottlo, but I bought a coke instead. I'm not sure I can promise I'll be that good next week.'

Jill said, 'You're in a different place than last week, hey Dean. I can see you feel really sad. Did something happen that you would like to talk about?

Dean said, 'Not really, different day, same crap.'

Jill said, 'Is now a good time for you to express how you're feeling?'

Dean shrugged. 'Just dark hey. I get up and go to work alright, but I don't want to go home. It just reminds me, y'know?'

'What's your compassionate self saying to your struggling self right now, Dean?' asked Jill.

'I have no idea,' he replied.

The group sat in silence. Amy noticed that it was a comfortable silence.

After a little while, Jill made another comment toward Dean. 'It's really hard to find your compassionate self when you don't think you deserve kindness, hey.'

Dean nodded. Amy guessed there was a back-story.

Jill continued, 'Dean it seems like it's tough to find your compassionate self when you're hurting self is so overwhelmed.'

He nodded again.

'Maybe you can only hear the depression voice at the moment.'

Dean was silent. Amy could sense that he agreed.

Jill turned her attention to the group. 'Guys that have been coming here a while, can we help Dean find his compassionate voice?'

Phillip started. 'All this time you've been there for us mate. You need to know we're here for you too; to help you get through this.'

Maddy added, 'I love hearing what you have to say, Dean. You're so smart, and you're kind as well. Like you don't make us feel dumb when you say something clever.'

Karen was smiling and nodding her head. 'Cookie would be lost without you. You treat that dog better than a baby!'

The group shared a smile.

Jill said, 'As I hear people say things like: you've been here for us; how much your dog means to you; how smart and kind you are; it seems to me that we're holding the parts of you that you can't hold for yourself at the moment.'

Jill left some space which no one filled. Amy could feel the care towards Dean and that the group meant something to Dean.

Jill asked, 'What do you do when you're feeling this way Dean?'

'Try to forget. Usually drink enough to forget.'

'What are some more compassionate things you could do?' Jill asked.

'I don't know. It just works for me to have a drink and forget.'

'Yes. It work's until it doesn't hey,' said Jill.

With a wry smile, Dean said, 'Even when I drink, I still can't stand myself and I feel pretty crook in the morning.'

Jill added, 'Not to mention how much harder it is to concentrate at work when you feel rough. So, what could you do instead? Something a bit more useful?'

'I don't know,' said Dean.

Jill asked Dean, 'Ok, what would you say to Keith if he wanted to do something other than drinking too much when he was feeling low.'

'What, like that forgiveness rubbish or something?' he scoffed.

The group waited for Dean.

'I don't know, maybe go for a walk or something. Maybe put on the TV?'

Jill said, 'There's your inner wisdom right there, Dean. It exists. It's just easier for you to access it for others at the moment that's all. We all need practice finding it for ourselves.'

Dean looked at the floor. Amy got the feeling that Dean wasn't quite convinced about what Jill was saying. He just looked defeated.

Jill took a breath. 'Hang on, Dean. I need to stop myself here. It seems I'm badgering you into doing something. What does that remind you of?'

'I guess my dad was always hassling me to get on and do stuff.'

Jill said, 'I kind of feel that sometimes you hassle yourself for being down and not doing something to feel better. And then I jumped in to asking you to come up with solutions as well. Let's go back to where you could only hear the depression voice. Let's try and work out what happens for you when the compassionate voice tries to get in.'

'Er,' I have no idea, said Dean.

'Would it be okay if we try a different process?' asked Jill.

Dean responded with a purposeful look and Amy felt his consent, trusting the group to support him. As the group worked together with Dean, he went on to share more about why he thought he doesn't deserve forgiveness. Amy found out that Dean's child, Anna, drowned in the local swimming pool while he was distracted talking to his mate. The group leaned into Dean's suffering and agreed that it was understandable to feel overwhelming regret in life. Some of the others disclosed their regrets. Amy found herself thinking *I wish I could go back in time too.*

At the end of their discussion, Dean reported feeling calmer and more hopeful. He told the group that he was going to ward off his depression by creating a new story. His home was going to be more than just past stories, it was going to be the holder of new stories too. He decided that when he felt like he wanted a drink, he would tell himself that it's normal to have such strong feelings about what happened. He also decided that instead of drinking, he was going to do some drawing when he got home from work each day.

When Jill quoted 'no sin makes a person ineligible for compassion' to Dean, Amy resonated with the quote so deeply that she felt compassion jump in her heart. Amy was beginning to see how she had dispossessed her compassionate self because she felt ineligible for kindness. She felt a tugging thrill as she saw how the group worked together and began to wonder if it could work for her too. The group dynamic gave Amy the idea that the people here are free to say whatever they want, and it's okay.

'I'll go next,' said Amy.

The group gave Amy their full attention. She still felt too ashamed to talk about her lack of confidence and too unsure to tell them about the pain in her chest. She decided to tell the story about Brogan.

She let it all out, concluding with '... and so this boss of mine, Brogan, just leaves me hanging.'

Jill responded first, 'Amy, it seems as though when you got the email, you weren't able to shrug it off and say to yourself, *I wonder what he wants, oh well I guess I'll find out later.*'

'No, I couldn't. I wish I could've. My whole day wouldn't have been ruined.'

Jill said, 'Yeah, there are a few thoughts running around my head. Are there some thoughts from the group before I say anything?'

Maddy said, 'I hate it when someone does that. I mean, how hard is it to say what it's about?'

Keith and Phillip were more than able to share in the frustration of the situation. Everyone has a boss to deal with at some point in their life.

Jill said, 'Perhaps at that moment, you blocked off all the positive, lovely things about you, which might have let you think that your boss could have equally wanted to see you for something good, not just something bad.'

'Yes,' said Amy. 'It didn't even cross my mind that it would be about something good.'

Joan had been listening intently. 'I can be a bit the same.'

Keith raised his hand gently.

Jill asks, 'Keith, is there something you would like to say to Amy?'

'Yeah, I'd like to offer some feedback,' said Keith.

Jill asks, 'Amy, are you open to feedback right now, or maybe wait for another time?'

'No, it's okay Keith,' said Amy.

'So when you got the email Amy, it seems like you could only see you're bad. Initially, you did well. You sent an email back to ask *what's this about*? You took action to help your suffering, which was your compassionate self responding. But when your boss didn't respond to your email, you went back to imagining you were at fault.'

Maddy said, 'Wow, Keith, that's so true!'

Keith smiles warmly at Maddy, and Amy enjoys wondering if Keith and Maddy like each other.

Amy felt so confident in the safety of the group that she went on to share how guilty she feels for letting her kids down. The group reflected to Amy that her guilt is actually the evidence of her love for her kids. In this way, Amy began to write her new self-compassion story.

Jill brought the session to an end, she impressed on the group how proud she was of each person for taking the time to show up, which was in itself an act of self-compassion.

Jill packed away the last chair and turned off the lights.

Reflections on the Group

Uncompassionate stories are learned and can be unlearned

As we begin to reflect on the characters in this group, we may see ourselves mirrored in their stories. This is what I love about group work. When we share our story, we give others permission to share their humanity, and we get to experience our own. Every experience of the other includes an experience of the self. Even if we have never experienced the exact same thing, we can be motivated by someone's story to move toward offering relief to their suffering.

Uncompassionate stories are learned. There are back-stories for all of the accounts that were spoken in the group. For instance, let's imagine that every time things were going great in Amy's family, something would make her mother mad, and the whole house would become gloomy. If we knew this back story then it would make sense to us that Amy might be afraid of feeling compassionate and happy because she has learned from her family story that when good feelings come, bad things are around the corner. This is important because the next time you are listening to someone, remember there are reasons for their words and behaviours. Let's go deeper into these stories.

AMY

What we did learn from Amy's old story is that her father would bring up her mistakes again and again. So, it's understandable that when she received the email from her boss that she began ruminating over the possible mistakes she might have made. It also stands to reason that Amy would assume an authority figure, Brogan, would be critical. Thus, if Amy does not wake up to the understanding that she has internalised her parent's critical voice, she will continue to be both victim and perpetrator of this critical spirit. When she does wake up to internalised critical voice, she can choose instead to give herself compassion and kindness.

MADDY

How we might respond to Maddy's situation is complex. Maddy's story is a teaching moment for us around judgement. When we move away from judgement, we are able to see that Maddy's responsibilities as a protective mother were torn. She is struggling to escape an abusive marriage, primarily because she doesn't feel it's safe for her and the kids to leave. Get away from the abuse, and they would be able to live freely for part of the time. However, she would regularly have to abandon the children to his unpredictable moods. If she stayed, Maddy thought at least then she would be there to protect them as much as she could.

While figuring out this dilemma, Maddy was oblivious to her uncompassionate self and found it difficult to stop and notice her own suffering. Maddy often said to herself that she was pathetic, useless and weak. In the same way that her abusive partner was keeping her stuck, her critical self was also keeping her stuck. But look at how the group responded to her struggle with compassion. We could see how committed they were to walk with her. The group provided Maddy with the opportunity to experience, and hopefully take on board, the embrace of shared humanity. What Maddy really needed in those moments of self-criticism was kindness, however, it will take a determined effort for Maddy to stop self-blame and offer compassion to her critical self.

DEAN

The story of Dean in our group reminds me of how people who are stuck in depression stories actively select and even evoke maladaptive storylines intrapersonally and interpersonally. People with depression tend toward recall bias [3], where recalled past and present stories hold more negative experiences than positive. Dean's back story is a difficult one. He has accumulated a whole pile of difficult stories. When Dean is overcome with pain, guilt and regret leading to his depression, it can be almost impossible for him to self-soothe or seek gentle support. This is where compassion from others in a group setting can be of great value. Accepting compassion from the group allowed Dean to wake up to the idea that, just like any other person, he is deserving of compassion. He deserved to lean in toward his own suffering.

Understanding Resistance in Allowing Compassion

There is a fight between compassion and criticism inside every one of us.
Who will win the battle is determined by how awake we are to the struggle.

We saw in the group that there are many reasons for resisting self-compassion. Perhaps one of the most prevalent learned stories believed is that self-compassion means weakness or self-indulgence. It would follow then that if Maddy did decide to extend compassion to herself, perhaps she would think she's letting herself off the hook. Another resistance story is one like Dean's. He believed that an action he committed was so bad that he did not, and will not ever, deserve forgiveness.

Many people don't think they are critical because they don't share their opinions with others.

Often, we can resist compassion by justifying self-criticism, 'Well, I'm critical because I care, or I want to make things better.' This may be true. Test it out. See if you're encouraged. Did Amy feel encouraged when she kept ruminating on the potential things she had done wrong? If criticism is constructive you will be helped by the comment and it will feel more like useful feedback.

When receiving feedback, you feel encouraged.
When receiving criticism, you feel discouraged.

When we are uncompassionately critical, we tend to zoom in on the negative details, and it's hard to take a step back and see the full picture. Self-compassion sees the whole picture and can offer perspective.

Waking up to self-compassion allows us to be more resilient. Resilience is the ability to return to normal after an upheaval. This is a difficult task in the absence of compassion. Without a person or group to talk to, unawakened old stories can leave us detached from compassion, which consequently separates us from kindness and understanding.

Being awake to self-compassion is easier for some more than others. Without early experiences of consistent love, it is difficult to practice self-compassion. It sure is easier to do anything when you have good role models. But even if you did not get the opportunity to witness a good role model, you can still learn self-compassion for yourself and towards others.

Sometimes we can find it difficult to even notice our own distress. Perhaps this is because we avoid the struggle involved in tolerating big feelings. Feeling more confident in our ability to be self-compassionate can make it easier for us to face our own suffering. If self-compassion is a battle for you, sometimes it's easier to find your compassionate voice by tuning into what we might say to others who are experiencing a tricky situation. For example, when you can't find your inner compassion, imagine someone else enduring the exact same scenario you are going through and think about something compassionate you could say to them. In other words, bring that inner wisdom that you would have used with the other person across to yourself. Perhaps begin with empathy, it allows you to acknowledge that you have a shared humanity with others and yourself.

There is no limit to what we can heal with and within God's love. Lean into your own suffering, knowing that His love in abundance will help you live in your new story around compassion.

Reflection

The way that we speak to ourselves changes everything. This is an opportunity for you to reframe the way that you speak to yourself from criticism to self-compassion.

Here are some phrases your compassionate self might reach out with to your hurting self:

- It's really tough going through this situation. Breathe. Slow breath in, slow breath out.
- There were underlying causes or unmet needs that led me to act in this way. I know I have to change. I'm working on it. I'll get there.
- Every normal person messes up badly from time to time.
- This is such an intense experience in me right now. It's okay to be very emotional and upset. When I'm ready, I'm going to do something to help me feel better, like to go for a walk or call a friend.
- Bad things are a part of the shared human experience. *Hurting one inside of me, you need to know that I am here for you when things are crap. Let me know what you need.*
- Because I am worthy of love, I'm not going to do something to harm myself.

Write in your journal about how this change of language helps you to be moved with self-compassion for yourself.

List a couple of situations where it is more difficult for you to be self-compassionate. Think about each one of those situations as if the situation belongs to someone else and ask yourself: What would I say to other people in a similar situation?

Shame Dialogues

Amanda

'We need never be ashamed of our tears.'

Charles Dickens

Have you ever felt shame?

Our world is throbbing with pain, and there is an enemy that wants to shut down humanity with a shame dialogue that holds us locked in a pattern of doubt and pessimism. Some days I struggle to find the words for the feelings that overwhelm and confuse my heart.

Bush fires, pandemics, tsunamis, economic recessions and stories of domestic violence roll across our screens with emergency announcements every day. Diagnosis after diagnosis, coupled with message after message of 'not being enough'. The news always reminds us that we are 'far from okay' and 'everything is not going to be all right'.

Shame, from knowing the truth, that maybe we don't really care what is happening out there hides around every corner and asks me to trust its predictions. Everything is falling apart and I don't even have the energy to show compassion to one more cause.

Did I say that out loud?

Can I shout it now?

I don't care! My heart is aching. I need to unpack my own story before I can listen with empathy to yours.

Can anyone hear me?

Noise shouts and chaos swirls with every scroll of our phones. Our world is throbbing with messages of despair. If we are not overwhelmed by the messages of fear and destruction, the responsibility of compassion for a world that is in pain weighs us down.

Shame.

Do more.

Be more.

Have more.

Care more.

Make a difference.

Be good.

Change the world.

Change yourself.

Be everything to everyone.

Never, ever, ever enough.

These are the shame dialogues that plague my heart and mind. They tell me I am not enough, I will never be enough, so why even bother.

Amid this shouting of fear, shame, and apocalyptic diatribe, there is a quiet conversation happening in coffee shops and church corridors that calls us to a place of rest and trust. Churches are compelling us to slow down and trust in a still, small voice.

There is a compassion revolution happening around the world.

How do I find the space for compassion in a world of so much pain and suffering?

How do I find space for compassion when I am shamed by the thought that I can never do enough?

Compassion asks us to lean towards a place of growth and understanding to move towards the suffering of another. We cannot go through a day in our culture presently without hearing a story of suffering.

During my study of compassion, I have come to realise there are foundational steps towards compassion.

The Steps of Compassion

The first step is to open our hearts and lives to the power of vulnerability. To be vulnerable is the way we can open up to the pain and discomfort of brokenness.

The next step is one of sympathy, which is to have the feelings of pity and sorrow for someone else's misfortune.

The third foundation of compassion is empathy. To be empathetic is to try to understand what another person is feeling. It sees the world through another's eyes.

We lean into compassion, as we learn to sit in the seat of the listener, not trying to do more, but to understand where they are coming from. It comes back to listening to one another's stories and giving each other the space to grow.

To be compassionate is to not only sit in the discomfort of the pain but to move forward into action to alleviate the suffering. It is difficult to truly be moved with compassion, if we are unable to firstly be compassionate to our own stories.

Jack Kornfield says, 'If your compassion does not include yourself, it is incomplete.'

In my story shame became the starting point of wanting to do and be there for others. If I could do more, if I could help more people, then somehow the deep mistrust I had with my own self worth, might go away. This shame, created deep places of fear in my life, that I would never be good enough.

My old story: I am not enough.

Self-compassion changes this story to a new one.

My new story: I am doing the best I can.

This reframing of my shame dialogue, started with my own self-discovery from the stories from my childhood. Scarcity was the foundation of this shame. I grew up thinking that we will never have enough money. I will never be enough for someone to love me. And what if there is not enough room for me to be myself.

This dialogue began with the scarcity mindset from my father's childhood, where he lived in poverty and his family had to work harder, to get more and more, to survive. My Dad rewrote his story. He reinvented his career many times over and provided enough for three children to go to private high schools and live an amazing life. This scarcity mindset, though, crowded every decision. It impacted my story.

My fear of not being enough or having enough called to the part of myself that thrived in the darkened corners of scarcity—whispering the worst-case scenario.

I am not enough.

I had to rewrite my story of enough-ness, with the pen of self-compassion.

As I started to understand where this shame dialogue of "not enough" came from, I could start to move with self-compassion into abundance. I had to start to believe what God said about me, about my worth, about his heart that is moved with compassion for my story. This is where compassion begins. In my relationship with God and understanding how much He loves me.

We cannot give fully give others compassion unless we understand our own story and are moved with compassion for ourselves. The way we think about ourselves and how we understand the love of God in our own circumstances changes the way that we understand the pain of another.

The way I have been learning to rewrite the stories of scarcity in my own life is through the lens of scarcity and then abundance. Scarcity is the hallmark of our media age right now. Threats and worry bombard us. The media (social media) thrives on this mindset. To combat this fear and scarcity that is very present, we need to move towards the opposite.

Recently I asked myself a simple question to live in a new story of enoughness.

'What is the opposite of scarcity?'

The answer was a simple word- abundance. Self-compassion shifted the atmosphere that held me locked in this shame dialogue and moved me towards abundance.

> *'And God can make all grace abound to you so that always having all sufficiency in everything; you may have an abundance for every good deed.'*
> *2 Corinthians 9:8 (ESV)*

Being moved with self-compassion is the way we rumble with the scarcity mindset of our culture and apply an abundant mindset in our everyday. It is not just about having a positive disposition saying everything is fine; everything is okay. It is a reframing of every thought that comes into our minds and filtering it through the lens of abundance.

Seeking abundance means to choose to believe that there is enough. Abundance asks us to choose to be fluid, not rigid in the outworking of daily life. It means to hold things lighter and to let go faster. Abundance asks us to lean towards ourselves with compassion and kindness, rather than control and anxiety. It is speaking with self-compassion to understand our own stories and where we are living stuck.

Shame plays in the ground in between scarcity and abundance. It had my story in a holding pattern of pessimism that kept me small and insecure. When I released myself through self-compassion, it awakened the possibility that there is so much more to help me live in my new story.

Scarcity says there will never be enough.
Abundance says there is always enough.

Scarcity competes with others.
Abundance collaborates with others.

Scarcity hoards its treasure.
Abundance shares of its bounty.

Scarcity holds onto wisdom.
Abundance shares freely.

Scarcity is suspicious.
Abundance offers to help.

Scarcity is resentful.
Abundance trusts and builds.

Scarcity is afraid of being replaced.
Abundance is choosing growth.

Scarcity dwells in the past.
Abundance believes the best is yet to come.

Scarcity thinks small.
Abundance thinks big.

Scarcity fears change.
Abundance is flexible, embracing change.

Scarcity complains.
Abundance encourages.

Scarcity thinks there is no room for me.
Abundance believes there is a massive wide space for everyone.

Scarcity excludes.
Abundance includes.

Scarcity gossips.
Abundance celebrates others.

Self-compassion is the language of abundance. It is speaking kindly with patience to myself. It is the capacity to give our soul the ability to breathe slowly and relax into the future with ease. Self-compassion will not lead us towards selfishness; it will help us to grow with strength and dignity.

Compassion is the language of God, the Father. It is a kind and merciful conversation that brings light into those shame-filled places. Like this scripture from the gospel of Matthew that draws us into an invitation of self-compassion.

> *'Are you tired? Worn out? Burned out on religion? Come to me. Get away with me and you will recover your life. |I'll show you how to take a real rest. Walk with me and work with me- watch how I do it. Learn the unforced rhythms of grace. I won't lay anything heavy or ill fitting on you. Keep company with me and you'll learn to live freely and lightly.'* Matthew 11:28 (MSG)

To live in freedom, awake to the calling that has been wooing you from places of restriction, we need to step into compassion for our own stories.

I have learnt that living awake is allowing myself to have the space I need to recover.

The voice that we speak to ourselves with is so often framed by the voices of authority in our lives. Our parents, amid their own failings, have imprinted our story with theirs. Our teachers, amid their own shortcomings, spoke things into our lives that hold us stuck. Our church pastors, amid their broken places, breathed shame into the crevices of our hearts.

Despite it all, there is an awakening happening in women across the earth, who are rewriting their story through self-compassion. We are learning to show ourselves the same kindness and understanding we give to others.

Our story matters.

What happened in those quiet and secret places is not unseen, when our story was difficult and traumatic.

We are important.

Read that sentence again.

Now read it through the lens of abundance and self-compassion.

I am important.

Somebody needs my story.

I believe, dear one reading this sentence right now, there are so many beautiful, deep and meaningful days to come.

As we grow in our capacity to reframe the shame dialogues and wake up to the story that is being rewritten in our days to come, we co-create with a Father God, who wants to bring out the best in our story—bringing all things together for good—weaving hope, light and truth into those places of darkness.

Reminding us of safe spaces, that we can return to when all seems lost.

This is living freely and lightly.
This is a place of safety.
This is the power of self-compassion.

Shame holds us often in a place of scarcity. Abundant thinking helps us lean towards self-compassion. As we awaken to the power of our own story and are moved with compassion for the child within, there is a reframing that happens.

Let's reflect now with compassion in your story.

How can I speak with compassion to myself today?

What area of my life am I coming from a place of scarcity?

What would my life look like in the future if I thought with abundance?

Write Your New Self-Compassion Story

Old Story: I am not competent.
New Story: I am doing the best I can.

Old Story:

New Story:

Hand Of Compassion

Anne

You've heard the saying 'put yourself in the other person's shoes.' What if we could put our critical, judgemental self into the shoes of our hurt and suffering self? We may find we would be more compelled to do something to compassionately relieve our own suffering.

Let's imagine you're suffering because you did something you wished you could take back, and you want to do something to help the self that is suffering. You want to speak words full of wisdom to offer yourself compassion, but you can't find them. Sometimes your yucky feeling is so big that it's too hard to think of the words to help balance out the suffering with compassion.

Let me share a simple technique I have found helpful.

- Place a hand on the part of the self that is in pain with the intention to offer comfort and compassion. It may be your heart, your stomach, your mind etc.
- Wherever it is, press in gently with a hand that says something like, 'I've got you' or 'Everyone makes mistakes' or 'It's okay, It's okay.' Find a gentle short phrase that works for you.
- Ask God's love to come into that hurting place. His anointing oil can flow into all those painful spots and bring healing.
- Then allow God's love to spread into all the hurting places, like a soothing balm, until you feel loving peace move through your body.
- Rest in Gods embrace for as long as you like.

Balancing Compassion

It is often said, 'I wouldn't treat a friend the way I treat myself.' Frequently in therapy, I hear clients being compassionate to others but not to themselves. Getting the harmony between compassion for self and compassion for others can be tricky. On the one hand we are told to reach out to others with compassion. On the other, we are told to do more for ourselves.

We need a balance scale where we are just as compassionate to our self as to others.

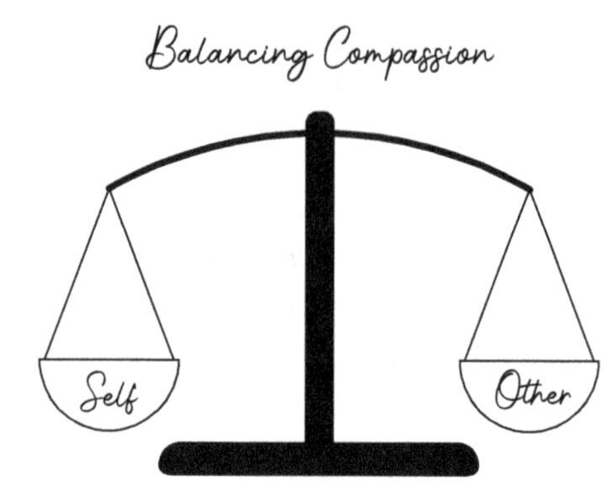

Often, I will use a balance scale, or a seesaw, to illustrate self-compassion imbalance.

I say, 'You are not more important or less important than other people.' Holding out both hands, I ask, 'Do you think you are being more, or less, compassionate to yourself than the other person in this situation?' People can then reflect and work out for themselves how they might need to balance the scale of compassion.

Tough vs Gentle

We also need a balance between gentle compassion and tough compassion. There are different ways of expressing compassion. One way is to be gentle and kind; such as forgiving yourself for saying the wrong thing. Another is to be tough, which can be the kind thing to do; such as saying 'No' when I want to eat an ice-cream, because I'm dairy intolerant. For me, the best way to know if I need gentle or tough compassion is to see what action best relieves suffering.

Write down three occasions where you have demonstrated compassionate acts. Perhaps you helped someone at the supermarket with his or her shopping bags.

Examine areas where you are compassionate toward others.

- How compassionate am I to someone in pain?

- How compassionate am I to someone living in poverty?

- How compassionate am I to some who is grieving?

Explore your relationships. Are you able to balance compassion toward others with care for yourself?

Your

Story

creative exercises

'To heal, we must consider not only our physical selves but our emotional ones as well. We must boldly draw back the curtains of our lives, and peek within. We must walk in our darkest rooms and turn on the light.'

Nicole Sachs

A great opportunity to explore and understand our stories is through creativity and insight. In this section of Awake, Anne and Amanda have created some creative exercises to help us find ways to rewrite our story.

Find a journal, open a new document on your computer and let's get creative.

The expression of telling our story, and learning from our story walk together hand in hand.

As we become more adept at telling our story creatively, we learn from the story and rewrite a new one into the future.

Have you ever dreamed of sharing your story one day to help others?

This part of the book is designed to help you do this with these four exercises that can be repeated over and over again to gain insight and clarity from your story.

- Drawing our life map.
- Writing your story
- Changing false beliefs.
- Understanding our dreams.

'You've got a new story to write. And it looks nothing like your past.'

Danielle La Porte

Writing is a powerful tool for insight and discovery; it is a vehicle for change. Words are not just for some. Writing is not just for the gifted. Books come to the diligent. Songs come to those who sit with blank pages before them. Creativity is just a tool; it is not some ethereal, magical being that only belongs to some.

The more we write, the clearer our communication comes. Journalling is a powerful tool for understanding your own narrative. Somebody needs your story, and the beginning part of it is your own self-awareness. As we learn to communicate our story, it becomes our teacher.

The way that we write our own story is by allowing ourselves the permission to fully explore the depths, heights of joy, and the troughs of despair. One way that you can begin today to understand your story is by drawing a life map. Put down this book and find a journal or a big piece of paper. Also, grab a pen or a big bag of markers.

The next step is to start to draw a line across the page that denotes the length of your life story. The line can wobble across the whole page, it can go in circles, or you can have a very straight line. Then begin at the beginning, and draw a small symbol that denotes a significant memory from your early years. It could be a time when you hurt yourself? Maybe you shifted house? What about a moment when something formational happened at school? Your first time on stage? Did you travel overseas?

Allow yourself the time to remember.

This can be a difficult exercise for those who have experienced trauma, so be careful and make sure you go and see a counsellor, therapist or psychologist if memories surface that are difficult. This also is a great opportunity to go back to your safe place that we talked about on page nine.

Seeing our lives across a map of symbols, stories, memories, and moments is a powerful tool for transformation.

Writing Your Story

'Heroes didn't leap tall buildings or stop bullets with an outstretched hand; they didn't wear boots and capes. They bled, and they bruised, and their superpowers were as simple as listening or loving. Heroes were ordinary people who knew that even if their own lives were impossibly knotted, they could untangle someone else's.'

Jodie Picoult

The next part of writing your story begins with this life map. Take each little moment you have found on this map and begin to write your memories down. Often people get stuck in writing their life story because they start with a blank page. The life map forms a framework of stories to help you unpack and discover a plan to write.

Start with the symbol or drawing you put on the life map.

Now begin with answering these questions.

My Story:

Write the story in a few words from your point of view. (Use I)

Their Story:

Write the story in a few words with a third-person point of view. (Use we or them)

The Lesson:

What is the lesson in the story?

Now write three opening sentences for this memory from your life map.

Choose your favourite sentence and begin to write about this memory from one of the points of views. You can write in first-person narrative, third person expressive writing or present tense, i.e. your own story or you could write your story as a fictional character.

'Everything is within your power, and your power is within you.'

Janice Trachtman

Each time we are asked to write a new story, often there is a tape from an old story that is holding us captive. In the midst of that moment, right at the very point of being asked to do something new, get curious, and write down what the old belief is telling you and let's together rewrite your future.

For example;

Tomorrow you are asked to share your story on a stage of 1,000 people sitting in the audience. The first thought that comes to mind?

Old Story

Write the old story statement here: (what first comes to mind)

Next, write the answer to these questions.

1. Is this old story the truth?

2. If it is the truth, can you change the meaning?

3. If this old story is not true and you can change it...what happens in your body when you believe the new story about this thought?

4. Where do you feel the tension?

5. Whose voice can you hear?

6. Is there someone in particular that is linked to this old story?

7. What images do you see? Memories, visions, dreams, nightmares?

8. What do you think God would say to you about this thought?

The answers to these questions will help you gain insight into where this old story stems from. As we face the truth of this old story, we can rewrite a new story.

New Story

Think about the scenario again. Tomorrow you have been asked to speak on a stage to 1000 people sitting in the audience.

What is the new story about this opportunity?

How can you speak with compassion to yourself about the fear you feel about this scenario?

Replace it with your new story that is filled with self-compassion.

Understanding Your Dreams

'Dreams are a reservoir of knowledge and experience, yet they are often overlooked as a vehicle for exploring reality.'

Tarthang Tulka

As we awaken to the power of our individual stories, often we will start to remember our dreams more and more. There is passage from the Bible that shows us the power of dreams:

> *'And it shall come to pass afterward, that I will pour out my Spirit on all flesh; your sons and your daughters shall prophesy, your old men shall dream dreams, and your young men shall see visions.'*
> *Joel 2:28 (ESV)*

Yesterday's stories can be trapped in our visioning, imaginings and dreams. The power of rewriting our stories and the future means that we can wake up to the meaning these internal conflicts are trying to resolve and live in our new story.

At the end of each day, we have a lot of information to process. There is so much that our body wants to move through, even just on a sensory level. Our brain unconsciously continues the work of making sense of reality; even while we sleep or rest. Images speak to us in dreams as our minds work through the data of our life. Dreams can provide powerful images for transformation to help us.

That's why sometimes we wake up and think more clearly about something. Our mind is still working in the background while we sleep. If we pay attention to dreams, they can give us information to release and re-story information. This is a helpful place to start your interest in awakening to your subconscious.

Set aside a journal specifically for visions, imaginings and dreams to discover themes and messages from God. Leave it next to your bed.

Steps to Help You Process Your Dreams.

1. Write down as much detail as you can as soon as you can.

2. Separate the dreams into the parts of the dream that has people you know and people you don't.

3. If the dream contains people you know, ask yourself what God is trying to show you about them or your relationship with them.

4. If the dream contains people you don't know, ask yourself what each person represents to you.

5. Write down the overall feeling you are left with from the dream. Is that a feeling you are experiencing throughout the day?

After three weeks of dream journal keeping, see if there is a theme amongst your dreams. God uses dreams to awaken us to His purpose in our lives and destiny.

Amanda

'Stories are a communal currency of humanity.'

Tahir Shah

'The sun rose with fierce colours in December that year. She sat on the floor that Christmas morning; awkwardly watching the family stumble in from their beds. As they rubbed the sleep from their eyes, they searched under the tree for the promise of presents. The tree sat empty, and she smiled happily, knowing where all those presents lay. She didn't say a word. She knew where the presents were, but her family awkwardly waited.'

What if we all woke up on Christmas morning with our family, and had bought presents, but they remained hidden at the back of our cupboards?

We smile and enjoy the moment, but our families and friends are wondering what is going on?

Imagine our changing story within, is like a little sack full of presents, stored ready for Christmas morning. Gifts hidden at the back of our cupboard.

Hiding. Waiting. Our stories should be shared. It is in the giving of those stories, that the joy of the moment is activated.

Words are our tools of resurrection. They are change agents. As our story is rewritten, we start to change the story of those people closest to us. Speaking encouraging words for others starts to flow naturally, from the places deep within. When we change the way we think, an awakening occurs.

The awkwardness of that Christmas scene is that we, the reader all know what happens next. The family knows that gifts are coming. The memory is not remembered until the gift is shared. This is the same as our stories. It is in the telling of our stories that the understanding is found. The movement created in this understanding is the awakening that we have been talking about throughout this book.

Recently at an event, I was asked to write postcards for random strangers. I sat out on a park bench at a campsite and began to write whatever encouragement came to my heart.

The beauty of encouraging words when you have no knowledge of the receiver is there is no preconceived bias in the way that you write. I have been the receiver of many such cards and encouragements over the years, and they have been so important in my journey. As I sat there writing for the group of people sitting inside, I was on to my tenth postcard, and my hand was tiring. Without thinking as I flicked through my Bible, read the first few words of this scripture and then thought that's a great verse to encourage someone with.

> *'Awake, O Sleeper! And Christ will give you light.'*
> *Ephesians 5:14 (ESV)*

I went on to write to this to a stranger, 'There is an awakening happening in your heart and life this season. Seek surrender to his ways.'

As I finished writing the postcard, I looked up at my new friend sitting across the bench from me writing cards also, and I said out loud 'Oh goodness, I just wrote the most random card. I am not even sure I should put it in the pile. I thought, should you write to someone 'Awake, O sleeper'? Laughing, I slipped the card amid the pile and shook my head, wondering what that little moment was all about.

Later that evening, I sat amid the room of hundreds of leaders and as the night was coming to a close, I was walking out of the room and saw one lonely card left on a seat. Everyone had taken the time within the meeting to pick up the postcard on their seat and read the encouragement that was left to them. Tears and smiles filled beautiful moments of connection as people read words shared by a stranger. I picked up the postcard that was left on that empty seat to read what little message of encouragement was waiting.

I laughed out loud.

The postcard said;

> *'Awake, O Sleeper And Christ will give you light.'*
> *Ephesians 5:14 (ESV)*

That moment of clarity on the park bench outside came back as a gift into my own life to remind me of my own awakening in rewriting my story. A gift given rather than hidden in the back of my cupboard.

This is the gift that comes when we allow moments of clarity and insight, through self-reflection and prayer, to mark our stories. We can discover ways to connect with others through encouragement and believing the best. We can be people of great strength and soft hearts. When we discover our light, amid very dark times, when we explore the power of our own voice and stories, transformation happens.

It's natural for us to believe old stories because they were told to us by the people that matter. At some point in time, we have agreed with these stories about us and made them our own. Stories of validation empower us. Stories of disapproval create wounds that may never completely heal. But what if, instead of attacking ourselves for living in myths we didn't create, we could catch, contain, and transform these erroneous tales. In this way we can relieve future generations from walking in our old story.

There is a scripture that speaks hope into my story every time I read it. The difficult part it also speaks of absolute devastation.

> *'God sent me to announce the year of his grace-*
> *A celebration of God's destruction of our enemies-*
> *And to comfort all those who mourn.*
> *To care for the needs of all who mourn in Zion,*
> *Give them bouquets of roses instead of ashes,*
> *Messages of Joy instead of news of doom,*
> *A praising heart instead of a languid spirit.*
> *Rename them 'Oaks of righteousness'.*
> *Planted by God to display his glory.*
> *They'll rebuild the old ruins,*
> *Raise a new city out of the wreckage.*
> *They'll start over on the ruined cities*
> *Take the rubble left behind and make it new.'*
> *Isaiah 61:2-11 (MSG)*

Words can rebuild ruins.

Words can bring hearts to life.

I have found in my own life, that the rewriting of old stories does not come without destruction. The word destroy comes from the root word of the story. De-story. The ashes, the destruction, the removal of the house that once stood strong, is part of the rebuilding process, to bring the foundations into a place of strength and renewal. It is difficult to build a strong, lasting house if the foundation is not set in stone.

All of us have some wonky foundations from our childhoods. It doesn't matter how seemingly brilliant they were, life cracks open the foundations in all of our lives at some point, and we realise that there are some dark places looming in all of our lives.

Let's come back to the life of Deborah where we began our journey.

Gender bias was extreme in that culture of the day. Deborah would have had to dig deep into negative stories to explore the possibility of writing a new future for her family and life. Women were not leaders in this culture, women were not warriors and they were expected to live very quiet and hidden lives.

In the Book of Judges, it is stated that Deborah was a prophet, a judge of Israel and the wife of Lapidoth. She rendered her judgments beneath a date palm tree between Ramah in Benjamin and Bethel in the land of Ephraim.

Deborah's story of victory in the book of Judges is an encouragement to us today to live in our new stories that God is calling us into. She stood alongside her male counterparts and she radically changed the course of history in the way that she lived out a new story.

In reference to her influence among both men and women scripture foretells this about Deborah;

> *'May all who love you be like the sun*
> *when it rises in its strength.'*
> *Judges 5:31 (NIV)*

The wrestle she must have endured to step into this place of leadership would have been fierce. You don't change history by doing the same as has always been done. Those who are willing to stand up and find their voice rewrite history. This confidence begins with understanding and grappling with our own stories.

The rewriting of our story sometimes feels like it is going back before it rebuilds again. Sometimes an awakening looks like a sharp decreasing, little fires everywhere - a burning down of that which belongs to an old version of you.

As you sit and reflect about your stories, and moments of waking up to our stories throughout this book, our hope is that it would speak life into your darkened places, and it would speak to the importance of your own story.

It is our hope that you will:

Know the essence of your identity.

Believe in your worth and beauty.

Understand your authority.

Be moved with self-compassion,

Have more tools to rewrite your stories.

This is your awakening.

Awake-

Live in your new story.

> *'Wake up, wake up, Deborah! Wake up,*
> *wake up, break out in song!'*
> *Judges 5:12 (NIV)*

1. Bowlby, J. (1958). The nature of a child's tie to his mother. International Journal of Psychoanalysis, 99, 265–272.
2. Gilbert, P. (2014). The origins and nature of compassion focused therapy. British Journal of Clinical Psychology, 53, 6-41. DOI:10.1111/bjc.12043
3. Bower, G.H. (1981). Mood and memory. American Psychologist, 36, 129-148.

About the Authors

The Therapist

Anne Galambosi is a Perth clinical psychologist, life coach, speaker, uni lecturer, business owner, wife, mother and grandmother. Co-founder of The Boardroom Retreat, Anne sees the need for leaders to grow in emotional intelligence whilst sustaining resilience. Leaders often seek out Anne for her knowledge and gift of insight. For many years she has coached leaders to unlock keys that transform culture, tap into the emotional energy, and 'read the play'.

The Writer

Amanda Viviers is an Author Public Speaker and Radio Presenter. With a double degree BA in English Literature, Comparative Literature and History. She is the author of eleven books, the most recent "Dear Creative Self". She is a presenter on radio across New Zealand and Australia and is the co-founder of kinwomen; a network created to inspire women to start conversations that matter. Driven by a passion for social justice, she loves supporting projects for children in developing countries. Wife of Charl and Mum of Maximus and Liberty. She lives a creative life, helping people find their voice.

CPSIA information can be obtained
at www.ICGtesting.com
Printed in the USA
BVHW081408300621
610774BV00003B/9

9 781636 256139